# HISTORY
# OF
# MUSIC

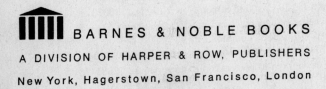

## by Hugh M. Miller

PROFESSOR EMERITUS OF MUSIC, UNIVERSITY OF NEW MEXICO

BARNES & NOBLE BOOKS

A DIVISION OF HARPER & ROW, PUBLISHERS

New York, Hagerstown, San Francisco, London

## About the Author

Hugh M. Miller received his B.A. from the University of Oregon and his M.A. and Ph.D. from Harvard University. Since 1947, he has been Professor of Music at the University of New Mexico, and from 1947 to 1957, Chairman of the Department of Music. He has been Professor Emeritus since 1973. During the academic year 1956–57, he was Visiting Professor of Music at the University of Oregon; in 1958, Fulbright Lecturer at Auckland University in New Zealand; and during the academic year 1965–66 he was Exchange Professor of Music at the University of Hawaii. In addition to having many articles published and belonging to a number of professional organizations, Dr. Miller is a popular lecturer on music. He is also the author of *Introduction to Music,* a companion Outline.

History of Music, Fourth Edition by Hugh M. Miller. Copyright 1947, 1953, 1960 by Barnes & Noble, Inc. Copyright © 1972 by Harper & Row, Publishers, Inc. All rights reserved. Printed in the United States of America. No part of this book may be used or reproduced in any manner without written permission except in the case of brief quotations embodied in critical articles and reviews. For information address Harper & Row, Publishers, Inc., 10 East 53d Street, New York, N.Y. 10022. Published simultaneously in Canada by Fitzhenry & Whiteside Limited, Toronto.
First Barnes & Noble Books edition published 1973
Library of Congress Catalog Card Number: 72–81476
isbn: 0 –06 –460147 –1

81    82    10

# Preface to the Fourth Edition

Since *History of Music* was first published in 1947, minor revisions and corrections have been made periodically, and the chapters dealing with twentieth-century music have been updated. The present edition is a completely rewritten and extensively reorganized work which takes into account numerous suggestions from readers and further experience in using the history as a textbook. The objectives of the Outline remain the same as before: concise presentation of basic essentials of music history in terms of broad stylistic periods, techniques, forms, schools, principal composers, and mention of representative compositions.

For references to recordings and scores at the ends of the first sixteen chapters, Arnold Schering's *Geschichte der Musik in Beispielen* has been deleted, and Carl Parrish's valuable *Treasury of Early Music* added.

Two new features will increase the value of the book: (1) inclusion of musical examples in score to illustrate certain technical problems, and (2) the use of photographic reproductions to illustrate basic types of notation discussed in Chapter 12.

It is hoped—and with modest feelings of confidence and optimism—that in its present edition the Outline will be an even more useful source of information than it has proved to be over the past quarter of a century.

The acquisition of historical information about music is of little value unless that information is applied directly to the literature of music. In any study of the history of music there is, inevitably, a considerable quantity of factual material that is of purely historical interest. However, in the present Outline, nonessentials, such as biographical detail, have been minimized or else eliminated altogether. The present emphasis is upon the organization and presentation of essential historical information that has a direct bearing upon the actual music of any given period, or else upon the development of musical trends. The Outline deals primarily with the characteristics of form and style as they apply to music of broad and specific periods, to nationalities or schools, and to the most important composers. This Outline, then, is intended to be a substantial guide to intelligent study of music by the amateur as well as by the advanced student of music. It can be applied equally well to the occupation of listening to records and to detailed analysis of musical scores.

Furthermore, the present work is more than a mere review outline. It is a functional work which can be used as the basic textbook in a college course in the history of music. This does not preclude collateral reading in the many excellent textbooks in general music history which are indeed valuable. But the present Outline should be the core of the study.

At the end of each chapter through baroque music, record lists have been provided. These are selected from available recordings including long playing releases, the *Anthologie Sonore*, and *2000 Years of Music*. As more and more representative works are issued, especially recordings of music prior to 1600, the lists should be supplemented.

Score lists, also, have been provided for representative music up to 1750, music for later periods being much more easily accessible. These lists are primarily based upon three musical anthologies: *Historical Anthology of Music,* 2 volumes, Apel and Davidson, 1947, 1949, Harvard University Press; *Geschichte der Musik in Beispielen* ("History of Music in Examples"), Arnold Schering, 1931, Breitkopf & Härtel (reprinted by Broude Bros., 1950); and *Masterpieces of Music before 1750,* Parrish and Ohl, 1951, Norton.

The author here wishes to express his deep gratitude to Dr. Lloyd Hibberd, North Texas State College, Denton, Texas, for his reading of the entire manuscript and for numerous invaluable suggestions and criticisms and to Mr. Walter Robert for reading proof.

# Abbreviations

HAM   *Historical Anthology of Music* (scores)

MM   *Masterpieces of Music Before 1750* (scores and records)

TEM   *A Treasury of Early Music* (scores and records)

# Table of Contents

# CHAPTER 1

# *Introduction*

The study of music history requires a preliminary understanding of some basic concepts and approaches.

**Interdependence of Music.** Music, like other arts, is not autonomous; it is always part of a total culture, both in time and place. Therefore, it is important to study music history against the backgrounds of social, economic, political, cultural, and philosophical developments.

**Relation to Literary Arts.** Music, as a form of human communication, from its earliest known beginnings has been closely associated with the literary arts: poetry, drama, and religious texts.

**Music Literature.** The study of music history is necessarily based on the study of music literature. Factual information is, of course, essential to history in any field, but unless that information is applied directly to the actual sound of music it is of negligible value. Thus, one must hear representative music of any era to understand that era musically. It is a great advantage to the modern student that there is a wealth of music authentically recorded and available for study.

A further approach to music literature is the study of musical scores. Modern editions and anthologies of early music enable the student to see in detail the various aspects of construction. Whenever possible, it is best to combine the visual aspect with the auditory, to "see" the music while hearing it.

**Kinds of Historical Information.** An adequate study of music history involves a coordinated knowledge of several areas.

*Forms.* The term *form* refers to the structural principles involved in musical composition. A given form is determined by a combination of these principles. The history of music is in part the history of ever-changing forms.

*Style and Technique.* Musical style is the composite of numerous techniques of composition involving the elements of melody, rhythm, harmony, texture, dynamics, and others. In certain periods of history, certain styles prevail. All eras, countries, schools, and individual composers have their own stylistic characteristics. Thus, one can speak of renaissance style, French style, Venetian style, or Beethoven's style.

*Medium.* In music, the term *medium* means the performing agent. In general, media are vocal, instrumental, or both; they are subdivided into various solo or ensemble combinations. The kinds of media employed in any given period constitute one indication of the kinds of musical sounds encountered at that time.

*Broad Categories.* Music history can be approached from the standpoint of broad categories of music literature such as religious music, secular music, dramatic music, symphonic music, and so on.

*Geographical Areas.* Music often develops differently in different regions, such as broad geographical areas, countries or cities. Music of a particular region is usually referred to as belonging to a *school.* Hence, we have such expressions as the Flemish school, the Italian school, or the Venetian school.

*Composers.* To know music history is to be familiar with the important composers and their contributions to music literature and the development of music. Sometimes a composer represents the culmination of a period ( J. S. Bach in the baroque era); sometimes a composer represents revolutionary innovations (Stravinsky and Schoenberg in the 20th century).

*Documents and Manuscripts.* Valuable contributions to music history have also been made by authors who have explained the musical practices of their own times. Such documents, many of which have been translated and published in modern editions, afford insight into music history.

Our present knowledge of earlier periods stems largely from

manuscripts in musical notation preserved in libraries and in museums throughout the world. The well-informed student of music history should know about them.

*Notation.* Since antiquity, music has been written down according to various systems of symbols called *notation.* How such systems developed is an important facet of historical knowledge (though such knowledge contributes little to the student's perception of musical sound). The advanced student must learn early notation for the purpose of transcribing manuscripts.

**Chronological Organization.** Music history, like the history of any other field, involves the chronological development of thought and practice from its earliest known beginnings to its present forms.

*Period Division.* The history of Western music is conventionally divided into eras, or periods of time. These divisions, which generally conform to similar eras in general history and the history of other arts, are referred to, respectively, as pre-Christian (Antiquity), medieval, renaissance, baroque, classical, romantic, and modern periods. Some eras are subdivided into early, middle, and late periods (early Renaissance, late Baroque, etc.), and subdivisions of major periods sometimes carry special names such as *Ars Antiqua* and *Ars Nova* of the Middle Ages.

Although period divisions are used for convenience in the historical organization of events and developments, it must be kept in mind that change from one period to the next does not take place suddenly. Evidence of change is invariably manifested before the beginning year of an era, and, conversely, the characteristics of an era continue long after it has ended. For example, evidence of baroque practices can be found at least two decades before the year 1600, when the baroque period is said to have begun, and renaissance techniques continued to be employed well beyond that year. Furthermore, no period in itself is static; changes take place continuously within a period.

# I

*Antiquity
and
Plainsong*

# CHAPTER 2

# Antiquity

Relatively little is known about the music of Antiquity (from prehistoric times to about A.D. 200). Well-established generalizations are that music existed in ancient civilizations and that our European musical heritage stems mainly from non-Western cultures in pre-Christian times.

## General Considerations

Before describing the principal musical cultures, we should answer these questions: Why is knowledge so limited? What are the sources of information? What are the theories concerning the origin of music?

**Limited Knowledge.** Much less is known about ancient music than about ancient pictorial art, architecture, or literature, for sound is an immediately perishable medium and its preservation depends either on the electromechanical means of recording of the 20th century or else on an adequate system of musical notation. Neither of these methods existed in Antiquity. What little music was preserved in notation before the birth of Christ is mostly indecipherable.

**Sources of Knowledge.** The limited information we have about ancient music has been gathered mainly from four sources: pictorial material, literary material, extant instruments, and ethnomusicology.

*Pictorial Material.* Pictorial representation of musical activity, especially that of people playing instruments, tells us something about the music of Antiquity. Drawings dating back to prehistoric times establish at least the existence of music.

*Literary Sources.* As long as man has had systems of written communications, he has recorded his ideas about music, rules of its construction, and its place in his society. Literary sources constitute our best information about ancient music.

*Extant Instruments.* A considerable number of instruments has been excavated from ancient caves, tombs, and temples. From such material, scholars are able to reconstruct instruments and sometimes even to determine the scales that were used. However, no one has been able to recreate the music which was once played on such instruments.

*Ethnomusicology.* Research dealing with primitive and non-Western systems of music is called *ethnomusicology.* It has provided some insight into ancient practices. By studying ancient cultures which still exist today (China, India, Arabia, etc.) and primitive cultures (such as those found among the aborigines of Australia, New Guinea, and South America), scholars have been able to project theories about ancient music.

**Theories of the Origin of Music.** We do not know precisely how or when music began, but there are some acceptable theories about its origin in prehistoric times.

*Communication.* In prehistoric times, man used primitive forms of drums and trumpets for communicating sound signals. He may have found these sounds pleasing to the ear and thus began to use them to create music.

*Dance and Work Rhythm.* Another theory is that music developed from the natural urge to accompany dance and work with some kind of rhythmic sounds, which gradually became musical creations.

*Emotional Expression.* Song may have evolved from the spontaneous vocal expression of anger, fear, anguish, and joy.

**General Features of Ancient Music.** Though we possess no definite knowledge of how ancient music actually sounded, we can make certain generalizations about the practice of music in ancient times.

*Dependency.* It is unlikely that ancient music was ever an independent art created solely for the pleasure of listening to it.

CHINESE CH'IN
(Zither Family)

HEBREW PSALTERY
(Zither Family)

HEBREW CYMBALS

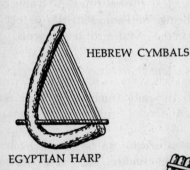

EGYPTIAN HARP

HEBREW SCHOFAR
(Trumpet Family)

GREEK PANPIPES

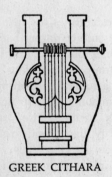

GREEK CITHARA

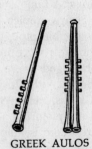

GREEK AULOS
(Single and Double)

GREEK
TYMPANON

Figure 1
*Some instruments of Antiquity*

Rather, it seems to have been an adjunct to other activities, such as dancing and ritual.

*Monophony.* It is generally believed that the music of Antiquity, like that of many primitive peoples today, was *monophonic;* that is, it was comprised of a single melodic line without accompaniment or harmonic support. In fact, music was almost entirely monophonic until about the 10th century A.D.

*Powers of Music.* Ancient man seems generally to have believed that music had mystic and magical powers capable of affecting his life, character, and well-being. References to this aspect of music are found in abundance in the literature of the ancients.

## Music of Ancient Cultures

Our knowledge of musical Antiquity comes both from non-European cultures and from the pre-Christian civilizations of Greece and Rome.

**China.** The history of Chinese music can be traced back at least 4,000 years. Philosophers and teachers, such as Confucius, indicated the important role of music in society and religion. The Chinese were probably the first to develop a science of acoustics and a theory of music. Chinese melody has long been associated with *pentatonic* (five-tone) scales.

**Egypt.** A wealth of pictorial evidence establishes the fact that music was an important part of Egyptian culture dating back to the fourth millennium B.C. A famous Theban tomb painting from the 15th century B.C. clearly depicts a group of musicians performing on harp, lyre, double pipe, and a lute-type instrument. These and other instruments were in common use. Instruments associated with Egyptian gods were the sistrum (rattle), associated with Isis, and flutes, with Osiris. Egyptian music strongly influenced that of the Greeks, Hebrews, and early Christians.

**Hebrew.** Although no pictorial material is preserved from ancient Hebrew culture, there is ample literary reference in the Old Testament to music, singing, dancing, and many kinds of instruments. Hebrew music was primarily religious and in the form of psalms which were sung in unison *responsorially* (solo singer answered by chorus) or *antiphonally* (two alternating choral groups). Various flutes, string instruments (psalteries), and percussion instruments were employed. The only ancient Hebrew instrument still employed today in synagogues is the shofar, a ram's horn trumpet.

**Greece.** Among the cultures of Antiquity, that of the Greeks has had the greatest influence on later theory, aesthetics, and musical concepts. The word *music* itself comes from Greece, as do many other terms, such as *tetrachord, lyric, rhythm, polyphony,* and *hymn.* Present knowledge of Greek music is based on a wealth of extant literature and pictorial evidence. Nevertheless, as for all Antiquity, there is a dearth of Greek music preserved in notation.

Greek music was inseparable from poetry and drama and was important in mythology and in ceremonial rites.

*Texture.* Like all ancient and primitive music, Greek music was largely monophonic, but the Greeks probably also practiced *heterophony,* in which the same melody is sung or played by two performers, one of whom elaborates it. It is also likely that there was some *magadizing* (performing a melody in octaves). This term derived from the Greek *magadis* (harp), which could be played in octaves.

*Doctrine of Ethos.* The ancient Greeks believed that music had a direct and profound influence on character. This theory is called the *doctrine of ethos.* Factors which determined a particular musical ethos were its rhythm, mode, and the instrument employed.

*Cults.* Two cults dominated musical concepts: (1) The cult of Apollo, which used the *kithara* (a plucked string instrument), was characterized by clarity and simplicity of form, objectivity, and restraint of emotional expression; (2) The cult of Dionysus, which used the *aulos* (a double-reed wind instrument), was characterized by subjectivity and emotional expression. These two concepts have had varying roles in the subsequent history of Western music, the former embodied in classical trends, the latter in romantic trends.

*Theory.* Greek theory was based largely on the acoustical mathematics of Pythagorean ratios. Scale patterns, called *modes,* were based on *tetrachords* (groups of four notes spanning the interval of a perfect fourth) which could be arranged in *conjunct order* (the highest note of the lower of two tetrachords being the lowest note of the tetrachord immediately above) or *disjunct order* (the highest note of the lower of two tetrachords being adjacent to the lowest note of the tetrachord immediately above). There were three genera of tetrachords: (1) the *diatonic* (e.g., the notes B C D E), (2) the *chromatic* (e.g., the notes B C C♯ E), and (3) the *enharmonic* (e.g., the notes B B♯ C E), where the first three notes are theoretically a quarter tone apart. The term *enharmonic* had a different meaning for the ancient Greeks than in modern usage where it denotes a different spelling of the same tone, for example F♯ being the same tone as G♭.

Another important aspect of Greek theory was the use of quantitative rhythms of poetry, called *rhythmic modes* (see Example 5, page 29).

*Notation.* The Greeks were among the first to develop systems of notation. There were two kinds: (1) an instrumental notation, the symbols for which were derived from Phoenician letters, and (2) a vocal notation, which consisted of symbols from the Ionic alphabet placed above the words of·the text.

*Instruments.* The principal instruments used, most of them borrowed from earlier cultures, were the *lyre* and *kithara,* which were small harps, *aulos, syrinx* (popularly known as *panpipes*), *krotola* (a castanet-like instrument), *tympanon* (a frame drum from which the word *timpani* comes), and *hydraulus* (water organ).

*Extant Music.* The few preserved examples of ancient Greek music are two Delphic Hymns to Apollo (c. 130 B.C.), two short Hymns to the Muse, a Hymn to Nemesis, and the Epitaph of Seikilos from the 1st century A.D. These remnants constitute a wholly inadequate basis upon which to judge the sound of Greek music.

*Writers.* Most of our knowledge about ancient Greek music comes from the writings of Terpander (c. 675 B.C.), Pythagoras (c. 500 B.C.), Timotheus (c. 450 B.C.), Aristoxenos (*Harmonics,* c. 500 B.C.), Aristotle, Plato (4th century B.C.), and Ptolemy (2nd century A.D.).

**Roman Music.** After Greece became a Roman province in 146 B.C., Roman music was largely derived from Greek music. The Romans contributed little to the development of music in theory or practice. Numerous reports indicate that large choral and orchestral performances were common in the first two decades of the Christian Era, and brass instruments were developed and used mainly for military purposes, but no Roman music has been preserved in notation.

**SCORES AND RECORDINGS**
   China: HAM 1
   Hebrew Music: HAM 6
   Greek Music: HAM 7

Christian song, variously referred to as *plainsong, plainchant,* and *Gregorian chant,* was the principal music of Western civilization for approximately a thousand years. In addition to the fact that it constitutes the largest and oldest single body of Christian music, plainsong is important because it was the main root of religious polyphony in the Middle Ages and Renaissance.

**General Characteristics.** Plainsong (1) is monophonic, (2) is *modal* (based on the church modes), (3) is normally sung *a cappella* (without instrumental accompaniment), (4) is *non-metric* (does not employ time signatures or bar lines), (5) uses free and flexible prose rhythms, (6) is *conjunct* (stepwise progression with few skips), (7) has a limited *range* (from the highest to the lowest notes of the melody), (8) was sung in Latin (is now often sung in translation), and (9) is written in a special *neumatic notation* (see page 68). An example of plainsong is on page 71.

**Origins.** Early Christian chant was borrowed from three especially important areas: (1) Byzantium (later Constantinople, now Istanbul) contributed a wealth of hymns; (2) Syria, a part of the Roman Empire near Palestine and the scene of significant religious activity, was noted for the development of antiphonal and responsorial singing; and (3) in Palestine, Hebrew chant was probably the most direct and extensive source of early Christian plainsong.

**Branches of Plainsong.** At various times during the first millen-

14

nium of Christianity, plainsong developed in five styles: (1) Byzantine chant, which continued to influence all plainsong, ultimately became the chant of the Greek Orthodox Church; (2) Ambrosian chant, named for Ambrose, a 4th-century bishop of Milan, is noted for its plainsong hymns and antiphonal singing; (3) Gallican chant was used by the Franks until the time of Charlemagne in the 8th century; (4) Mozarabic chant, which was used in Spain, was influenced by the Moorish invasion of the Iberian Peninsula in the 8th century; (5) Gregorian chant, a term often used for all plainsong, is named for Gregory the Great, a 6th-century pope who was largely responsible for organizing existing plainsong into a unified body. Ultimately, Gregorian chant came to dominate all Western plainsong as Rome became the center of Western Christianity.

**The Church Modes.** The theory of plainsong, which evolved during the early Middle Ages, is based on a system of scales known as *modes*. The eight church modes are divided into two classes: *authentic* and *plagal* modes.

**Authentic Modes.** The authentic modes have an *ambitus* (melodic range) from the *final* (the plainsong "tonic" and the final tone of a plainsong melody) to about an octave above it. The four authentic modes have Greek names: *Dorian,* with a final D; *Phrygian,* with a final E; *Lydian,* with a final F; and *Mixolydian,* with a final G.

**Plagal Modes.** The plagal modes have the same ambitus as the authentic modes, but they range from approximately a fourth below to a fifth above the final. The four plagal modes have the same finals as the corresponding authentic modes and use the prefix "hypo": *Hypodorian,* with a final D; *Hypophrygian,* with a final E; *Hypolydian,* with a final F; and *Hypomixolydian,* with a final G.

**Mode Number.** These eight church modes are conventionally numbered so that the authentic modes are the odd-numbered modes and the plagal modes are the even-numbered modes: (1) Dorian (2) Hypodorian (3) Phrygian (4) Hypophrygian (5) Lydian (6) Hypolydian (7) Mixolydian, and (8) Hypomixolydian.

**Other Modes.** Four additional modes are occasionally found in plainsong. These are the *Aeolian* and *Hypoaeolian* modes, with a final A (the same as the natural minor scale), and the *Ionian* and *Hypoionian* modes, with a final C (the same as the major scale). Although not recognized by the Church until the 16th century, these four modes existed as a result of *musica ficta* (accidentals or altered notes). For example, the use of the note B♭ in the first and second modes would produce the natural D minor scale, and the same note used in the fifth and sixth modes would produce the F major scale.

**Mixed Modes.** It is not unusual to find the plagal and authentic forms of a mode used in the same plainsong which ranges from several notes below the final to an octave or more above it.

**Styles of Text Setting.** *Text setting,* the relationship between the plainsong melody and text, is divided into four categories: (1) *syllabic,* where one note of the melody is set to one syllable of the text—typical of plainsong hymns and sequences; (2) *neumatic,* where a few notes of melody are set to one syllable of text—the most common style; (3) *melismatic,* where many notes of melody are set to one syllable of text—used in settings of the Alleluia; and (4) *psalmodic,* where there are numerous syllables on one repeated note—used in settings of the Psalms. It should be noted that a plainsong may shift from one style of text setting to another, but usually one style predominates.

**Tropes and Sequences.** From the 9th to the 12th centuries two new forms of plainsong were created: *tropes* and *sequences.*

**Tropes.** A trope is a phrase of text inserted syllabically into the melodic line of a plainsong. The text was either added to a melismatic passage or else a new melody was composed to the interpolated text. Example 1 illustrates the form of a trope. The words "Christe eleison" ("Christ have mercy upon us") are the original words of the plainsong. The words (in italics) *"Dei forma virtus*

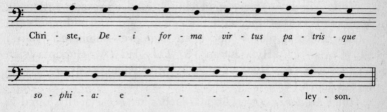

*Example 1. The form of a trope*

*patrisque sophia*" ("form, strength, and wisdom of God the Father") are the inserted text of the trope, set syllabically to the originally melismatic passage of the plainsong. Note also that characteristic plainsong style is monophonic, modal (Dorian), *a cappella,* and nonmetric, and that it uses free rhythm, narrow ambitus (a perfect fifth), conjunct progression, and the Latin language.

The most famous composer of tropes was Tuotilo (d. 915), a monk who resided at the Swiss Abbey of St. Gall.

**Sequences.** A special kind of trope called a *sequence* (Latin: *sequela* or *sequentia*) was created by adding texts syllabically to the *jubilus* (a long melismatic passage) of an Alleluia. The sequence had an indefinite number of sections beginning with a single line of text and melody, then a series of pairs of text lines with the same melody, and concluding with a single line of text and melody. Thus, the sequence form can be represented by the formula *a bb cc dd . . . n.* Sequences were later used as separate plainsongs, apart from the Alleluia. Probably the most famous sequence is the *Dies Irae* of the Requiem Mass.

Notker Balbulus (c. 840–912), a contemporary of Tuotilo at St. Gall, is the earliest known composer of sequences. Other composers were Adam of St. Victor (12th century), St. Thomas Aquinas, and Jacopo da Todi (13th century).

**The Roman Catholic Liturgy.** Because of its close association with music, first in the form of plainsong and later in polyphonic settings, the basic organization of the Catholic Service should be understood. It consists of two main divisions: the *Divine Offices* and the *Mass*.

**The Divine Offices.** The eight services celebrated at certain times of the day are called *Divine Offices*, or *Canonical Hours*. They are Matins, Lauds, Prime, Terce, Sext, Nones, Vespers, and Compline. The most important Offices employing music are Matins, Lauds, and Vespers.

**The Mass.** The Roman Mass is divided into two main parts: the *Proper* of the Mass and the *Ordinary* of the Mass. The Proper, which contains the variable portions of the Mass, includes six sections which use music. These are the *Introit, Gradual, Alleluia, Tract, Offertory,* and *Communion*.

The Ordinary, which contains the five invariable portions of the Mass, includes the *Kyrie, Gloria, Credo, Sanctus,* and *Agnus Dei.* Musical compositions entitled "Mass" are invariably settings of the Ordinary. Such works include Palestrina's *Missa Brevis* and Bach's *Mass in B Minor.*

**Requiem Mass.** The *Requiem Mass* [also called *Missa pro Defunctis (Mass for the Dead)*] is a special funeral Mass which includes sections from the Ordinary (Kyrie, Sanctus, Agnus Dei) and the Proper (Introit, Offertory, and Communion). It also contains a 13th-century sequence, *Dies Irae.*

**SCORES AND RECORDINGS**
  Antiphon and Psalm: MM 1, HAM 11
  Alleluia: MM 2, HAM 13
  Kyrie: HAM 15
  Kyrie with trope: HAM 16
  Sequence: MM 3, HAM 16
  Gregorian Gradual: HAM 12
  Gregorian hymn: TEM 4
  Byzantine chant: HAM 8
  Ambrosian chant: TEM 1, HAM 9, 10
  Gallican chant: TEM 2
  Mozarabic chant: TEM 3

# II

*The*
*Middle*
*Ages*
*(800–1400)*

# CHAPTER 4

# Secular Song

The period from the 9th to the end of the 14th centuries is referred to as the Middle Ages. In music history it includes some late developments in plainsong (see chapter 3), the rise and growth of polyphony (see chapters 5 through 8), and the first great literature of secular song, which is the subject of the present chapter.

Secular song undoubtedly played an important role in medieval society, but relatively little of it has been preserved. Both secular song and poetic creativity flourished mainly in France and Germany during the Middle Ages.

**Characteristics of Secular Song.** Secular song was stylistically more diversified than plainsong, and it had a number of distinguishing traits: (1) Like plainsong, it was monophonic. Although pictorial evidence suggests that secular songs may have been performed with some kind of improvised instrumental accompaniment, the manuscripts contain only single-line notation. (2) Unlike plainsong, it was metrical and mostly in triple meter. (3) It had stronger and more regular rhythm and employed recurrent short rhythmic patterns. (4) It had clear phrase and sectional structure with repeated sections and refrains. (5) Secular song was generally modal, but it favored the major (Ionian) and minor (Aeolian) modes. (6) It was generally syllabic. (7) It was mostly in the vernacular languages as opposed to the Latin of plainsong. (8) Secular songs dealt with a wider range of subjects than plainsong.

**Latin Songs.** A sizeable literature of Latin songs, called *conductus,* was created from the 10th to the early 13th centuries by vagrant students and minor clerics called *goliards.* Conductus dealt with a variety of subjects: love, drinking, political satire, ribald themes, and humorous paraphrases of plainsong. A famous conductus is *The Song of the Sibyl* from the early Middle Ages.

**Entertainers.** Minstrels of a low social order were called *jongleurs* in France, *Gaukler* in Germany, and *gleemen* in England. They roamed Europe in the Middle Ages, entertaining the feudal courts with juggling, card tricks, trained animals, and songs composed by others. Although they were neither poets nor composers, they were important musically because they kept alive and disseminated a large song literature.

**French Secular Song.** The largest body of medieval secular song came from two classes of French poet-composers: *troubadours* and *trouvères,* both terms meaning "finders." They were educated and cultured noblemen, mostly residents in the feudal courts.

*Poetic Types.* Troubadour and trouvère poetry is classified according to the following subject categories: (1) *canso,* a love poem, (2) *sirventes,* a satirical poem, (3) *planh,* a plaint or lament on the death of an eminent person, (4) *pastourelle,* a song, often in dialogue form, between a knight and shepherdess, (5) *chanson de toile,* a spinning song, (6) *enueg,* a satirical poem, (7) *aube,* the song of a friend watching over lovers until dawn, (8) *tenso* or *jeu-parti,* a poem in dialogue, and (9) *chanson de geste,* an epic chronicle, the most famous of which is the 11th-century *Chanson de Roland.*

*Music Forms.* The lines of distinction among the numerous song forms are less clearly defined than those among the poetic types, and there is considerable diversity of structure within each type. Recurrent sections of text and melody, called *refrains,* were common to several forms. One of these, which carried over into later polyphonic music, was the *virelai,* constructed according to the formula:

| phrase | 1 2 3 4 5 6 7 8 | | phrase | 1 2 3 4 5 |
|---|---|---|---|---|
| text | *a b c d e f a b* | or | text | *a b c d a* |
| melody | *A B c c a b A B* | | melody | *A b b a A* |

(Capital letters indicate refrains)

Another popular form was the *rondeau*, with the sectional plan:

| phrase | 1 | 2 | 3 | 4 | 5 | 6 | 7 | 8 |
|--------|---|---|---|---|---|---|---|---|
| text | *a* | *b* | *c* | *a* | *d* | *e* | *a* | *b* |
| melody | *A* | *B* | *a* | *A* | *a* | *b* | *A* | *B* |

The chanson de geste employed simple melodic formulae re-peated throughout the long poem. The *ballade* employed several different structures similar to the rondeau and virelai in the use of refrains.

*Troubadours.* The troubadours flourished in Provence in southern France from the end of the 11th to the end of the 13th centuries. Approximately 2,600 poems and some 260 melodies have been preserved. Some important troubadours were Marcabru of Gascony (d. c. 1150), Bernart de Ventadorn (c. 1127–95), Guiraut de Borneil (c. 1150–1220), Guiraut de Riquier (d. 1294), and Bertrand de Born (12th century).

*Trouvères.* The trouvères flourished in northern France slightly later than the troubadours. They produced some 4,000 poems, 1,400 of which have been preserved with melodies. Some important trouvères were Quesnes de Béthune (c. 1150–1226), Blondel de Nesle (c. 1150–1200), King Thibaut IV of Navarre (1201–53), and Adam de la Hale (c. 1235–85), the last and most famous trouvère, who wrote a medieval play with music entitled *Jeu de Robin et de Marion.*

**German Secular Song.** French troubadour and trouvère songs became the models for German poet-composers, *minnesingers* and *meistersingers,* from the 12th to the 16th centuries.

*Minnesingers.* The minnesingers ("love singers"), who flourished from the 12th to the 14th centuries, produced a literature of German poetry and song (*Minnelied*) dealing with a variety of subjects, including those of a quasi-religious nature. Minnesongs were usually in duple meter. The most typical form was a structure in three sections, *A A B* (called *bar form*), in which a melodic phrase (*Stollen*) was sung, then repeated with a different line of text, and this was followed by a different melodic phrase (*Abgesang*). The principal minnesingers were Walther von der Vogelweide (c. 1170–1230), Neithardt von Reuenthal (c. 1180–1240), Heinrich von Meissen (nicknamed "Frauenlob," d. 1318), and Heinrich von Mügeln (14th century).

*Meistersingers.* The successors to the minnesingers were the

meistersingers (master singers), who flourished in the 15th and
16th centuries and who were members of middle-class guilds
rather than the aristocracy. Their music, called *Meistergesang*,
was created according to strict rules. Bar form was the standard
structure. The principal meistersingers were Conrad Nachtigall,
Sebastian Wilde, Adam Puschmann (1532–1600), and Hans
Sachs (1494–1576), the most famous of all, who was immortal-
ized in Wagner's *Die Meistersinger von Nürnberg*.

**Other Countries.** The development of secular song was relatively negligible in areas outside France and Germany. In England, the Anglo-Saxon classes of *scops* (resident minstrels) and
*gleemen* (traveling minstrels) produced a limited song literature,
little of which has been preserved.

In Italy the nonliturgical religious *lauda,* a song of praise to
the Virgin, was composed in the Italian *ballata* form which
corresponds to the French virelai (*A b b a A*).

In Spain a similar form, the *cantiga,* also extolled the Virgin
and employed the same sectional structure, which in Spain was
called *villancico*.

**SCORES AND RECORDINGS**
Conductus: HAM 17
Troubadour song: TEM 6, HAM 18
Trouvère song: MM 4, HAM 19
Minnelied: MM 5, HAM 20
Meistergesang: HAM 24
Italian lauda: TEM 8, HAM 21
Spanish cantiga: TEM 7, HAM 22
English songs: HAM 23

# CHAPTER 5

# Early Polyphony

Probably the greatest single development in the entire history of music was the advent of polyphony toward the end of the first millennium of the Christian era.

**General Historical Background.** Charlemagne was crowned emperor in 800. The early Middle Ages (sometimes called the Dark Ages) to about the end of the 10th century witnessed the initial decline of the Holy Roman Empire. The 11th century contained a number of important events: the final schism between the Eastern and Western Churches (1054), the Norman Conquest of England (1066), the First Crusade (1096), the beginning of scholastic philosophy, the first translations of Arabic and Greek literature, and the rise of Romanesque architecture.

**Origin of Part Singing.** It is not known when part singing began. A prototype was the ancient Greek practice of heterophony. It is generally believed that different parts singing the same melody an octave apart (magadizing), in thirds (*gymel* or *cantus gemellus*, "twin song"), and perhaps in other intervals (4ths and 5ths) was practiced in secular song before it was known in church music. The earliest reference to part singing was in the 8th century. The known developments in polyphony from the 9th through the 13th centuries took place in church music and were based on plainsong.

**Organum.** The term *organum* is used in various stages of polyphony from its beginning to about the middle of the 13th century.

*Parallel Organum.* The earliest form of polyphony, first clearly described in the late 9th century, consisted of two voices moving in parallel motion. A plainsong melody, called *vox principalis,* was doubled at a fourth below by a second voice, called *vox organalis.* Either or both voices could also be doubled at the octave (*composite organum*) to create three- or four-part music.

At about the same time it was prescribed for two-part organum that the voices begin on a unison; then, while the vox organalis remained stationary, the vox principalis moved upward until the interval of a fourth was reached, after which the parts proceeded in parallel motion until cadential points where they converged to the unison (see Example 2).

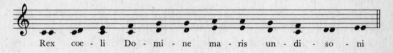

Rex   coe - li   Do - mi - ne   ma - ris   un - di - so - ni

*Example 2. Parallel organum*

This practice suggested the possibility of melodic independence in part writing and led to the next stage in development.

*Free Organum.* In the 11th century, strict parallel organum was replaced by *free organum* in which oblique and contrary motion between the voices was added to parallel motion, giving the two parts melodic independence. The intervals were predominantly fourths, fifths, and octaves. The organal voice was added above the plainsong, which was usually a trope. The two parts, moving in note-against-note style, still lacked rhythmic independence (see Example 3).

Cun - cti   po - tens   ge - ni - tor   de - us

*Example 3. Free organum*

The Latin expression *punctus contra punctum* (note against note) was the origin of the term *counterpoint.*

*Melismatic Organum.* In the early 12th century a new type emerged. It is referred to variously as *melismatic organum, sustained-tone organum, organum purum,* or *St. Martial organum.*

A plainsong, or section thereof, was assigned to one voice in long sustained notes to which was added a higher voice in faster moving note values (see Example 4).

Cun - - - cti po - - - tens

*Example 4. Melismatic organum*

This stage of polyphonic development thus achieved both melodic and rhythmic independence.

**Writers and Documents.** Among a number of treatises dealing with practices of organum, the most important are: (1) an early reference to part singing by Bishop Aldhelm (c. 640–709), (2) an anonymous treatise entitled *Musica Enchiriadis*, and (3) a commentary on it entitled *Scholia Enchiriadis*, both in the 9th century and constituting the first clear description of organum, (4) *Enchiridion Musices* by Odo de Cluny (d. 942), a theoretical treatise in the first half of the 10th century, (5) the most important writings of Guido d'Arezzo (c. 995–1050) in the first half of the 11th century, and (6) the writings of the so-called John Cotton (11th to 12th century), which describe the contrapuntal techniques attained by the early 12th century.

**Manuscripts.** The most important manuscripts are the *Winchester Troper* (11th century), which contains tropes in organum, and the manuscripts of *St. Martial* (Limoges, France) and *Santiago di Compostela* (northwestern Spain), which contain melismatic organa of the early 12th century.

**SCORES AND RECORDINGS**
  Parallel organum: MM 6, HAM 25
  Free organum: MM 7, HAM 26
  Melismatic organum: MM 8, HAM 27
  Gymel: HAM 25c

The century and a half from approximately the middle of the 12th to the end of the 13th centuries is commonly known as the *Ars Antiqua* (the Old Art), as it was referred to by musicians in the 14th century. It was an era of further significant developments in polyphony.

**General Historical Background.** This was the time of the Crusades, the building of the Gothic cathedrals, chivalric poetry and song, the rise of European universities, the high point of medieval scholasticism, and the economic, political, and social system known as feudalism. Some important names are St. Francis of Assisi, Roger Bacon, St. Thomas Aquinas, Frederick II of the Holy Roman Empire, and Louis IX, king of France from 1226 to 1270.

**General Musical Characteristics.** The geographical center of music was Paris. The names of the first truly important composers appeared. Polyphony continued to develop mainly under the auspices of the Church, but independent secular forms of polyphony appeared.

*Polyphony.* Polyphony was mainly three part, though two-part writing continued and four-part writing was introduced. Parts were generally in the same register so that crossing of parts was characteristic. Imitation was rare and incidental. A greater degree of rhythmic and melodic independence among parts was manifested. *Cantus firmi,* borrowed or derived from plainsong, continued to be the principal basis of construction.

**Meter and Rhythm.** Two time factors dominated secular monophony and polyphonic forms: *triple meter* and *rhythmic modes.* Triple division of notes, called *tempus perfectum,* resulted in metric schemes which would be the equivalent of $\frac{3}{4}$, $\frac{6}{8}$, or $\frac{9}{8}$ time when transcribed into modern notation.

**Rhythmic Modes.** The medieval rhythmic modes consist of six patterns of long ( – ) and short ( ᴗ ) units. According to medieval theorists these modes, labeled with Greek names, were patterns of three or six beats (see Example 5).

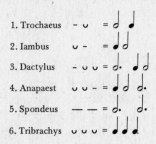

*Example 5. The rhythmic modes*

In actual practice only the first three modes were commonly used. There was some flexibility in the use of modes, for the patterns did not remain rigidly the same, and even the mode itself sometimes changed during the course of a melodic line.

**Harmony.** All harmonic intervals were employed: fourths, fifths, and octaves still predominated, but dissonant intervals (seconds and sevenths) became prominent and were not restricted by rules of usage as they came to be in the Renaissance.

**Other Characteristics.** Although instruments were certainly employed, they were not indicated in the music. It is probable that parts or passages without texts were played instrumentally and that instruments sometimes doubled vocal parts.

**Forms.** New forms developed in the Ars Antiqua were Notre Dame organum, polyphonic conductus, motet, hocket, rota, and rondellus.

**Notre Dame Organum.** Organum, as developed in the Notre Dame School in Paris in the second half of the 12th century, evolved from St. Martial (melismatic) organum. It consisted of sections in melismatic style with both parts sung by solo voices, alternating with sections of plainsong sung by a choir. The new feature of this organum was the appearance of sections in *discant style* in which the tenor was in shorter and measured notes. Such a section was called a *clausula* (plural *clausulae*). Clausulae generally corresponded to the parts of plainsong which were themselves melismatic. From the beginning of the 13th century, the melismatic sections of organum were gradually replaced by discant style. Organa were composed in two-part textures (*organum duplum*), three-part textures (*organum triplum*), and four-part textures (*organum quadruplum*). Example 6 illustrates a fragment of organum duplum followed by the beginning of a clausula section on the syllable "Do" of "Domino."

*Example 6. Organum duplum and clausula*

**Polyphonic Conductus.** *Polyphonic conductus,* not to be confused with the earlier monophonic conductus, flourished principally in the first half of the 13th century. Unlike organum, the parts moved together in similar rhythm, and the tenor part was originally composed rather than borrowed from plainsong. The texts were nonliturgical and set mostly in syllabic style, as shown in Example 7.

*Example 7. Polyphonic conductus*

Polyphonic conductus were composed in two, three, and four parts. Conductus style was also employed in secular forms such as ballades and rondeaux.

**Motet.** During the second half of the 13th century, the *motet* became the principal polyphonic form, gradually replacing organum and conductus. It originated in the process of adding words—the French *mot* means "word"—to the duplum (upper) part of a discant clausula. This part was called the *motetus,* a term which came to be applied to the entire composition. The 13th-century motet was constructed according to the following steps: (1) a plainsong was selected for the tenor (lowest) part; (2) it was modified according to one of the rhythmic modes; and (3) above it were added two parts (*motetus* and *triplum*) in faster moving notes. These parts carried different texts, religious or secular or both, in Latin or the vernacular. Since the tenor part carried no text other than the initial word or words (called *incipit*) of the plainsong melody, it was probably played on an instrument. As in other medieval polyphony, triple meter was a typical feature, as were also the occasional clashes of dissonant intervals. The motet style of the 13th century is illustrated in Example 8.

*Example 8. Thirteenth-century motet*

**Hocket.** Hocket (also *hoquet* or *hoketus,* meaning "hiccough") was a device frequently found in late 13th- and 14th-century polyphony. A melodic line was frequently interrupted by rests which alternated between two voice parts as shown in Example 9.

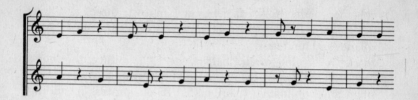

*Example 9. Hocket*

Although hocket appears in virtually all medieval forms, a composition which used the device extensively was called a hocket.

**Rota.** The *rota* is a canon or round in which two or more parts carry the same melody at different times. Isolated examples of this form appear in the Ars Antiqua. The most famous rota is *Summer is icumen in* which probably dates from about the middle of the 13th century.

**Rondellus.** The *rondellus* (not the same as rondeau) was a secular form, usually in three parts, employing the principle of *exchange* in which three different melodies (*a, b, c*) were exchanged among the parts according to a rotational plan such as the following:

$$
\begin{array}{ccc}
a & b & c \\
b & c & a \\
c & a & b
\end{array}
$$

The parts begin together rather than consecutively as in the rota.

**Composers.** Notre Dame composers Leonin (or Leoninus) in the late 12th century and Perotin (or Perotinus) in the early 13th century composed organa, polyphonic conductus, and motets. Petrus de Cruce (or Pierre de la Croix) composed motets in the late 13th century. Franco of Cologne, author of a late 13th-century treatise on notation, was also an important composer of motets.

**Manuscripts.** Leonin's *Magnus Liber Organi* is a collection of two-part melismatic organa for the entire church year. The most important manuscript is the *Montpellier Codex,* which contains 345 medieval compositions, mostly motets. Other manuscript collections are the *Bamberg Codex,* containing 108 three-part motets and *Las Huelgas Codex,* containing organa, conductus, and some 58 motets.

**SCORES AND RECORDINGS**
    Notre Dame organum with clausula: MM 9, TEM 9, HAM 28c
    Clausula: HAM 28d, 28e, 30, 31
    Polyphonic conductus: MM 11, HAM 38, 39
    Motet: MM 10, TEM 10, 11, HAM 28h, 32, 33, 34, 35
    Hocket: TEM 11

# CHAPTER 7

# Ars Nova

The 14th century in music is referred to as the *Ars Nova* (the New Art). While it represents the end of the Middle Ages in music, it also foreshadows some renaissance trends.

**General Historical Background.** The decline of feudal aristocracy and the rise of urban middle classes began in the 14th century. It was also the beginning of separation between church and state and between religion and science. Political dissension in the Church resulted in authority divided between two papacies, in Rome and Avignon (1378–1418). It was the century of the Great Plague (1348–1350), and the beginning of the Hundred Years' War (1337–1453) between France and England. Giotto, a Florentine painter, was the most famous artist of the period. Significant literary activity reflects the thought and spirit of the period in the works of Petrarch, Dante, Boccaccio, and Chaucer.

**General Musical Characteristics.** (1) Musical leadership was shared by France and Italy. (2) Far more secular than sacred music was composed. (3) *Tempus imperfectum* (duple division of notes) was used more often than tempus perfectum. (4) The rhythmic modes were abandoned in favor of more complex and diversified rhythms. (5) Cantus firmus was less often used; more music was entirely composed without borrowed material. (6) There was a distinct trend toward melodic and rhythmic interest centered in the top voice. (7) Thirds and sixths appear more frequently as harmonic intervals in accented positions. (8) A melodic formula, commonly known as the *Landini cadence*, consists of the scale-degree pattern 7–6–1 (hence, more correctly called a *7–6–1 cadence*). It appears in several different forms in 14th- and early 15th-century music (see Example 10).

*Example 10. Landini cadence*

### The French Ars Nova

The Ars Nova in France was an evolutionary extension of the Ars Antiqua more than was the case in Italy. Nevertheless, new forms and techniques were developed. In general, rhythmic complexity was more evident in France than in Italy.

**Forms.** The polyphonic motet continued to be written in France, but with important changes. Equally important were new polyphonic secular forms: ballade, rondeau, and virelai. Continuing the traditions of the trouvères, monophonic songs also were composed.

**Isorhythmic Motet.** The most important cantus-firmus form of the 14th century was the *isorhythmic motet,* which evolved from the 13th-century motet. The tenor part employed a plainsong in much longer and more diversified patterns, called *talea,* which replaced the rhythmic modes of the earlier motet. Repeated melodic sections, called *color,* did not necessarily coincide with the talea. The isorhythmic principle was also applied to upper parts, but less often and less strictly. The isorhythmic motet continued the practice of using different texts in the upper parts and passages of hocket.

**Ballade.** The *ballade* consisted of several stanzas, each with the same music, according to the sectional formula *AAB* in which the first section (*A*) was repeated with different text and different endings. Ballades were mostly three-part compositions with melodic and rhythmic interest in the top voice.

**Rondeau.** The polyphonic *rondeau,* not to be confused with the rondellus, derived from the monophonic trouvère form and followed the formula *ABaAabAB,* with a recurrent refrain (*A*) having the same words and music. Rondeaux were composed in two, three, and four parts, but most commonly in three parts for solo voice with two lower instrumental parts in slower moving rhythms.

**Virelai.** The *virelai*, also called *chanson balladée* in the 14th century, was, like the rondeau, derived from the monophonic trouvère form with the sectional plan *AbbaA* for each stanza of the poem. Most chansons balladées were monophonic, but many polyphonic compositions were also written in this form.

**Composers.** The leading composer of the French Ars Nova was Guillaume de Machaut (c. 1305–77), who was also an eminent poet. His compositions represent all the French forms of the time, and, typically, he wrote more secular than sacred music. However, his longest and most celebrated composition is the *Notre Dame Mass*, which was the first complete polyphonic setting of the Ordinary by one composer. In four-part texture, it employs the isorhythmic principle in all but the Gloria and Credo.

Philippe de Vitry (c. 1290–1361), also a poet-composer, is known primarily for his treatise on notation entitled *Ars Nova* (c. 1325), from which the entire 14th-century musical practice took its name.

**Works.** In addition to the Machaut *Mass*, other important works of the period are: (1) the *Roman de Fauvel*, a satirical poem which contains 130 interpolated compositions of various types including some isorhythmic motets, (2) the *Mass of Tournai* (c. 1300) containing a complete setting of the Ordinary, but whose sections were probably composed at different times by different composers, (3) *Ars Novae Musicae*, a treatise by Johannes de Muris (c. 1290–c. 1351), and (4) another treatise, *Speculum Musicae* (*Mirror of Music*), by Jacques de Liège (c. 1270–c. 1330), also dealing with 14th-century musical practices.

## The Italian Ars Nova

Italian polyphonic music came prominently into the picture for the first time. The principal distinguishing features were that (1) it did not employ cantus firmus technique; (2) it was less rhythmically complex than French music; (3) it employed simpler textures; and (4) it introduced a characteristic florid vocal style.

**Forms.** Three secular forms dominated the Italian Ars Nova: madrigal, caccia, and ballata.

*Madrigal.* The earliest Italian polyphonic form was the *madrigal,* usually in two vocal parts. Each stanza in duple time concluded with a *ritornello* section in triple meter.

*Caccia.* The *caccia,* which flourished from about 1345 to 1370, was the first musical form to exploit the principle of *canon* based on continuous imitation between two or more parts. Two upper parts were sung in strict imitation at the unison and with a long time interval between the first and second parts. The third and lowest part was freely composed in slow-moving notes and was probably played on an instrument. Caccias usually had a canonic ritornello section at the end.

*Ballata.* The *ballata* (not to be confused with the French ballade) originated as a dance song, and it developed somewhat later than the madrigal and caccia. Its sectional structure resembled the French virelai with refrains, called *ripresa,* sung at the beginning and end of each stanza (*AbbaA*).

**Composers.** The principal composer of the Italian Ars Nova was Francesco Landini (or Landino, 1325–97). He was a blind organist in Florence who composed over 140 two- and three-part ballate, some twelve madrigals, and one caccia. Other composers were Jacopo da Bologna, Ghirardello da Firenze, and Giovanni da Cascia (also known as Johannes de Florentia).

**Documents and Manuscripts.** The *Pomerian* by Marchetto of Padua is an early 14th-century treatise which first established the acceptance of tempus imperfectum. The most important manuscript collection is the *Squarcialupi Codex* which contains some 350 compositions, mostly two- and three-part pieces representing twelve 14th- and 15th-century composers.

**SCORES AND RECORDINGS**
   *French Ars Nova*
      Machaut Mass (Agnus Dei): MM 13
      Isorhythmic motet: HAM 43, 44
      Ballade: HAM 36, 45, 47, TEM 17
      Virelai: HAM 46
      Rondeau: HAM 48
   *Italian Ars Nova*
      Ballata: MM 14, HAM 51, 53
      Caccia: TEM 16, HAM 52
      Madrigal: HAM 49, 50, 54

# CHAPTER 8

# Medieval Instruments and Dances

Pictorial and literary sources establish the fact that instruments were widely used in the Middle Ages. However, little purely instrumental music has been preserved in notation and there are no known composers of instrumental music.

**Instruments.** There were many medieval instruments; only the principal kinds are listed here.

*Bowed Instruments.* The most important bowed-string instruments were *vielles*, the ancestors of the renaissance viol family. The *rebec* was a pear-shaped instrument. The *tromba marina* of the later Middle Ages was a long, single-string instrument, or it had two strings tuned in unison.

*Plucked Strings.* The most important instrument in this class was the *lute*, which had a pear-shaped body and angled neck. The *psaltery*, an instrument of the zither class, had a flat sounding board.

*Wind Instruments.* End-blown flutes were called *recorders*. The *shawm* was a double-reed instrument. Various types of horns and trumpets were in common use.

*Organs.* A small portable organ was called a *portative organ,* or *organetto.* A medium-size, nonportable organ was the *positive organ,* important because it was probably the first organ for which polyphonic music was composed. In the 14th century, still larger organs (up to 2,500 or more pipes) were built for churches in Europe. The earliest organ music preserved in notation is in the *Robertsbridge Codex* (c. 1325).

SATAN PLAYING A VIELLE
(13th Century)

ANGEL PLAYING A REBEC
(13th Century)

JONGLEUR PLAYING
A VIELLE
(15th Century)

A PLAYER ON THE
TROMBA MARINA

*Adapted from* A History of Music by Emil Naumann

Figure 2
*Some instruments of the Middle Ages*

*Other Keyboard Instruments.* Keyboard instruments of the harpsichord and clavichord types were not in general use until the 15th century.

*Percussion Instruments.* Drums of various sizes and shapes were used mostly for dance music and military purposes. Kettle drums used in pairs were called *nakers*. The principal cylindrical drum was the *tabor*. Various kinds of cymbals and bells were also employed.

**Uses of Instruments.** Medieval composers were not concerned with specific media. Whether a composition was to be performed wholly or partly by instruments was never indicated, nor were specific instruments named in a score. Medieval practice can be described in terms of five ways instruments were probably used: (1) Textless parts in polyphonic music were probably intended to be played by instruments as, for example, in 13th-century motets and 14th-century cacce and ballate. (2) Instruments were used to double one or more vocal parts. (3) They may have been substituted for voices in one or more parts with texts. (4) Vocal polyphony was occasionally played entirely by instruments. (5) Music clearly intended for instrumental performance was mainly dance music and a few instrumental motets and conductus.

**Medieval Dance Forms.** Almost all of the relatively few dances preserved are monophonic pieces. Folk and court dance music was mostly improvised or played from memory. The *estampie* (also *estampida, istanpitta, stampita*) was the principal 13th-century dance form, usually in triple time, and with repeated sections corresponding to repeated dance patterns. Other dances were the *danse royale*, and the 14th-century Italian *istanpitta* and *saltarello*. A dance in three or four sections was called *ductia*. A concluding section of a dance piece, with change of meter, was variously called *rotta, rotte*, or *rota*, which terms were also used to designate a canonic form and an instrument.

**SCORES AND RECORDINGS**
　Estampie: MM 12, HAM 40
　Danse Royale: HAM 40a, 40b
　Ductia: HAM 41a, 41b
　Saltarello: HAM 59b
　Instrumental Motet: TEM 11
　Organ estampie: HAM 58

# III

*The
Renaissance
(1400–1600)*

# CHAPTER 9

# The Fifteenth Century

The 15th century witnessed the final transition from the Middle Ages to the Renaissance, a transition which was reflected in the arts, literature and philosophy. The centers of musical activity shifted from France and Italy to England and the Netherlands.

**General Historical Background.** Medieval feudalism was replaced by urban culture. Humanism, the dominant philosophy of the Renaissance, became firmly established. Important historical events were the English victory at Agincourt (1415), the fall of Constantinople (1453), the close of The Hundred Years' War (1453), and the discovery of America by Columbus (1492). The invention of movable type in 1454 was ultimately to have a profound effect on the dissemination of music. Art, literature, and music flourished in the Burgundian courts under the patronage of the dukes Philip the Good (1419–67) and Charles the Bold (1467–77). Famous artists of the time were Ghiberti, Donatello, Leonardo da Vinci, Botticelli, Van Eyck, and Raphael.

## English and Burgundian Music

The first half of the 15th century was dominated by English and Burgundian composers.

**General Musical Characteristics.** (1) There was a preponderance of three-part polyphony in the early 15th century. (2) Melodic and rhythmic interest was characteristically in the top part. (3) Many of the compositions were in effect solo songs

with textless (instrumental) parts below. (4) Melodic progress-
sion was characterized by numerous thirds (see Example 11).

*Example 11. Melodic progression*

(5) Triple meter was more commonly employed than in the 14th
century. (6) There was a marked trend toward *chordal style* (also
called *familiar style*). (7) Passages of parallel sixth chords (first-
inversion triads), called *discant* in England and *fauxbourdon*
on the Continent, were typical, as illustrated in Example 12.

Lau - da - mus  te.   Be - ne - di - ca - mus  te.   A - do -

*Example 12. Discant or fauxbourdon*

(8) Cantus firmi were less frequently employed than in Franco-
Flemish music after 1450. (9) Imitation was infrequently used.
(10) The Landini cadence (7–6–1 cadence) was still quite
common.

**Forms.** The basic musical forms found in the first half of the
15th century were essentially those of the late Middle Ages, but
new styles and techniques evolved.

*Mass.* Polyphonic setting of the Ordinary of the Mass became
a standard liturgical form. Composers sometimes employed
plainsong tenor parts, and they also began to use secular tunes as
cantus firmi.

*Motet.* The isorhythmic motet was still used occasionally, but
it was gradually replaced by styles emphasizing the top voice,
or else a chordal texture including the use of fauxbourdon.

*Carol.* A popular 15th-century form in England was the two-part *carol.* It was sung to a religious poem of numerous stanzas with the same music and a refrain called a *burden.*

**Secular Polyphony.** The main type of secular music during the entire 15th century was the *polyphonic chanson,* which used secular texts in French. Most chansons were like solo songs, with the principal melody in the top part. The most common sectional structure was that of the rondeau (ABaAabAB) with recurrent refrains (capital letters).

**Composers.** The principal English composer of the first half of the 15th century was John Dunstable (c. 1370–1453). Others were Lionel Power (d. 1445), "Roy Henry" (probably Henry V, 1387–1422), Cooke, and Thomas Damett. The continental composers of the Burgundian school were Guillaume Dufay (c. 1400–1474) and Gilles Binchois (c. 1400–1460).

### Franco-Flemish Music

Although Burgundian composers continued their creative activities well past the middle of the century, the Franco-Flemish school came to the fore in the late 15th century. Its techniques spread throughout Europe, establishing a style which later dominated 16th-century music.

**General Musical Characteristics.** (1) Four-voice writing became more fashionable from the middle of the century. To the tenor, heretofore the lowest part, now was added a lower part. Thus, the conventional designation of parts, from top to bottom, was *cantus* or *superius, altus, tenor,* and *bassus.* (2) There was more stylistic equality among parts, creating a balanced polyphony. (3) Imitation played a more prominent role than ever before. (4) New types of canons were created. (5) Fauxbourdon and Landini cadences disappeared. (6) Pairing of voices in alternating passages, called *duet style,* was a common procedure. (7) Passages alternating between chordal style on the one hand and rhythmically diversified counterpoint on the other were typical. (8) Authentic (V I) and plagal (IV I) cadences became more common than modal cadences. (9) In general, composers of the late 15th and early 16th centuries initiated a more expressive style, called *musica reservata.*

**Forms.** Franco-Flemish composers developed new techniques rather than new form types.

**Canon.** Canonic form, first exploited in the 14th-century caccia and abandoned in the early 15th century, now became important in the late 15th century. In addition to canons at various pitch and time intervals of imitation, new canonic devices appeared: (1) *augmentation* (increasing the time values of the notes in the imitating voice), (2) *diminution* (decreasing the time values), (3) *mensuration canons* (several voices carrying the same melody at different rates of speed), (4) *inversion* (ascending intervals imitated by descending intervals and vice versa), (5) *retrograde motion* (the imitating voice progressing backwards, called *cancrizans* or *crab canon*), (6) *double canons* (in four parts with two different melodies, each canonically imitated), and (7) combinations of these devices. Canons were employed mainly in settings of the Mass and in some motets.

**Mass.** In addition to canonic settings of the Mass, called *prolation Mass,* another type was the *cantus firmus Mass* or *cyclical Mass,* in which the same melody was used for each successive section of the Ordinary. These cantus firmi were usually plainsongs, but secular tunes were also used, the most popular of which was "L'Homme Armé," used by composers from Dufay to the end of the 16th century. Masses were usually given the title of the cantus firmus (for example, *Missa L'Homme Armé* or *Missa Salve Regina*). Masses not based on a cantus firmus were called *Missa Sine Nomine.* Still another procedure, called *soggetto cavato,* was the construction of a theme derived from the vowels of a name or phrase. For example, in Josquin's Mass *Hercules Dux Ferrarie* the vowels from the name were converted into syllables to become the subject (see Example 13).

re    ut    re    ut    re    fa    mi    re

*Example 13. Soggetto cavato*

**Motet.** Motets were composed for the Proper of the Mass and some of the Offices. Cantus firmi were used less often in motets than in polyphonic settings of the Ordinary. Franco-Flemish motets often included sections in chordal style, duet style, fugal or imitative style, and in free nonimitative counterpoint. Changes from one style to another corresponded to divisions of the text.

**Secular Music.** The chanson continued to be the principal type of secular music. It became less sectionalized, as in the earlier rondeaux and virelais, and had a more continuous structure. Monophonic and polyphonic secular songs, in Germany called *Lieder* (singular *Lied*), flourished from the late 15th century to the end of the 16th century.

**Composers.** The principal Franco-Flemish composers of the late 15th and early 16th centuries were Antoine Busnois (d. c. 1492), Johannes Ockeghem (c. 1430–95), Jacob Obrecht (c. 1450–1505), Josquin des Prez (c. 1450–1521), Heinrich Isaac (c. 1450–1517), Pierre de la Rue (c. 1460–1518), Alexander Agricola (c. 1446–1506), and Loyset Compère (c. 1455–1518).

## Manuscripts and Documents

A number of important collections belong to the 15th and early 16th centuries. The *Old Hall Manuscript* contains Masses and motets by English composers. The *Trent Codices* in six volumes contain 1,585 compositions by some seventy-five composers of the 15th century. The first collection of motets for the entire church year, by Isaac, is entitled *Choralis Constantinus* (early 16th century). The first printed music, the *Odhecaton*, published in Venice by Ottaviano dei Petrucci (1466–1539) in 1501, contains late 15th-century polyphonic chansons. The first dictionary of musical terms, *Terminorum Musicae Diffinitorium* (c. 1475), was compiled by Johannes Tinctoris (c. 1445–1511), a noted theorist, composer, and commentator on the music of his time. Important collections of German monophonic and polyphonic secular music are *Liederbücher* (song books) of *Lochamer, Munich,* and *Glogauer.*

**SCORES AND RECORDINGS**
*English*
  Motet: TEM 18, HAM 61, 62, 64
  Mass: HAM 63
  Secular music: HAM 85, 86

*Burgundian*
  Motet: HAM 65
  Mass: MM 15, HAM 66
  Chanson: HAM 70
  Ballade: HAM 67
  Rondeau: HAM 68, 69, 71, 72
*Franco-Flemish*
  Motet: MM 18, 19, HAM 76, 90
  Mass: HAM 73, 77, 92, 106
  Canon (Mass): MM 17, HAM 89
  Chanson: MM 20, HAM 91
  Virelai: HAM 74, 75
  Rondeau: HAM 79
  Polyphonic Lied: HAM 87

# CHAPTER 10

# The Sixteenth Century

The Renaissance reached its culmination in the 16th century. It was an era of great achievements in all the humanities. In vocal polyphony it represents one of the pinnacles of attainment in the history of music.

**General Historical Background.** Humanism was the pervading philosophy of the century. The Protestant Reformation and the Catholic Counter-Reformation dominated religious history. Noted monarchs of the century were Charles V and Philip II of the Holy Roman Empire, Francis I of France, and Henry VIII of England. It was a period of exploration; some famous explorers were Sir Francis Drake, Cortes, Magellan, De Soto, Balboa. Two notable events were the Council of Trent (1545–63) and the defeat of the Spanish Armada in 1588. The impressive roster of illustrious names in Italian and Germanic art includes Leonardo da Vinci in the early 16th century, Cellini, Michelangelo, Titian, Tintoretto, Veronese, Dürer, Grünwald, and Holbein. In science, Copernicus and Galileo are the most famous names. Literature is represented by the Dutch theologian and humanist Erasmus; Machiavelli in Italy; Rabelais, Montaigne, and Ronsard in France; Cervantes in Spain; and Shakespeare, Spenser, and Bacon in England.

**General Musical Characteristics.** (1) Although Franco-Flemish techniques continued to dominate both sacred and secular music throughout Europe, other national schools emerged in the course of the century. (2) Vocal polyphony reached its ultimate degree of perfection. (3) Vocal style was dominant, but the beginning of an independent instrumental style was evident. (4) Religious music was still dominated by the Roman Church, but Protestant music, principally in Germany, France, and England, began an ascendancy which reached its culmination at the end of the Baroque. (5) Secular music rose to a new eminence under the patronage of the nobility. (6) Modality still influenced both sacred and secular music, but the trend was strongly toward major and minor tonalities. (7) A sense of harmonic completeness pervaded 16th-century music with its triadic structure. (8) Textures varied from chordal to fugal and were generally characterized by balanced polyphony with equality of parts.

## Roman Catholic Music

Forms and styles of liturgical music, founded by the Franco-Flemish composers in the early 16th century, had a continuous and widespread development throughout the century.

**General Characteristics of Style.** (1) Equality of parts was the characteristic texture. (2) The number of parts ranged from three to eight or more, but five-part texture was the most common. (3) Full triadic texture gave a rich harmonic sonority to the music. (4) As in the 15th century, chordal style often alternated with sections in fugal style. (5) Treatment of dissonant intervals was strict and confined to the following devices: passing tones, neighboring tones, anticipations, suspensions, and cambiatas (see Example 14).

*Example 14. Treatment of dissonance*

The dissonant intervals were seconds and sevenths between any two voices, and fourths between the lowest sounding voice and any other. Passing tones, neighboring tones, anticipations, and the dissonant tone in cambiatas always appeared in rhythmically weak positions; the dissonance of a suspension always appeared on a strong beat. (6) Although instruments were undoubtedly used in performance, the music was written *a cappella* with no instruments indicated. (7) The music was mostly diatonic, but chromaticism began to appear late in the century. (8) Latin continued to be the language of the Roman Church, but vernacular languages were occasionally used outside Italy.

**Forms.** Masses and motets continued to constitute the main body of religious music. Some nonliturgical religious forms also belong to the period.

**Mass.** Cantus firmus Masses on plainsongs and secular melodies and *sine nomine* Masses were the principal types. Another form, which began in the late 15th century, was the *parody Mass*. In this form, a complete motet or a secular chanson was musically altered to fit the text of the Ordinary. Composers borrowed from their own or other people's compositions. Complete canonic Masses were less common after the early 16th century.

**Motet.** Motet construction did not change appreciably from the techniques employed by the Franco-Flemish composers early in the century. In fugal motets each successive phrase of text introduced a new theme or motive which was then imitated in other voices. Divisions of the text from one line to the next, called *points* (or *points of imitation*), overlapped so that in one or more voices a new line of text was introduced with a corresponding new

*Example 15. Overlapping point*

theme or motive before the preceding line of text was concluded
in other voices. This procedure is illustrated in Example 15, an
excerpt from the motet *Ave Maria* by Josquin. One line of text
ends with the word "mulieribus" and the next line begins with
"et benedictus" accompanied by a new theme introduced in the
bass and imitated in successive voices. Overlapping points such
as this gave a marked continuity to the form.

Example 16, an excerpt from the beginning of a motet by Jacob
Handl (Latin, Gallus, 1550–91), illustrates a typical shift from
strictly chordal style on the words "Ecce quo modo moritur" to a
cadential measure of rhythmically independent counterpoint on
the syllable "ju" of "justus" and back to chordal style at the
conclusion of the cadence.

*Example 16. Change of texture*

*Nonliturgical Forms.* Religious songs of praise, called *laude*,
were given simple polyphonic settings in chordal style. The texts
were sometimes in Latin, other times in Italian.

**Schools and Composers.** Despite the continued influence of
Franco-Flemish composers, there were important regional schools
of Catholic liturgical music.

*Franco-Flemish School.* Important musical posts throughout
Europe continued to be held by Franco-Flemish composers.
Among these the best known were Orlando di Lasso (also
Orlandus Lassus, c. 1532–94), Philippe de Monte (c. 1521–
1603), and Clemens non Papa (c. 1510–58).

*Roman School.* At the head of Catholic music in Rome stands

Pierluigi da Palestrina (c. 1525–94) whose name is traditionally synonymous with the perfection of sacred polyphony. His successors were Marc Antonio Ingegneri (c. 1545–92), Felice Anerio (c. 1560–1614), and Giovanni Nanino (c. 1545–1607).

*Spanish School.* Cristóbal Morales (c. 1500–53) and Tomás Luis de Victoria (c. 1549–1611) were the principal Spanish composers. Their music reflects an intense religious fervor and at the same time a characteristic stark quality.

*Venetian School.* The most notable feature of the music by composers at the Church of San Marco in Venice was the use of impressive antiphonal effects produced by separate choirs (*cori spezzati*). Adrian Willaert (c. 1490–1562), a Flemish-born musician, was the founder of the Venetian school. Late renaissance music, foreshadowing baroque style, was composed by Andrea Gabrieli (c. 1510–86) and his nephew Giovanni Gabrieli (1557–1612).

*English School.* An extensive literature of Catholic Masses and motets was created by English composers, most of whom also wrote Protestant and secular music. The leading name among these is William Byrd (c. 1543–1623). Earlier composers were John Taverner (c. 1495–1574), Christopher Tye (c. 1497–1573), Robert White (c. 1534–74), and Thomas Tallis (c. 1505–85).

*German School.* Catholic Church music did not flourish in Germany, mainly because of the Protestant Reformation. Nevertheless, there were several illustrious German composers who contributed substantially to Catholic literature: Ludwig Senfl (c. 1490–1543), Jacob Handl, and Hans Leo Hassler (1564–1612), a product of the Venetian school who wrote polychoral music.

## Reformation Music

Perhaps the most cataclysmic event in the history of the Christian Church was the Protestant Reformation in the 16th century. Although church music was dominated by Roman Catholicism during the century, Protestantism also stimulated musical creativity.

**Germany.** The Reformation movement dates from Martin Luther's *Ninety-Five Theses* in 1517, and subsequent political and theological attacks on the Roman Church. A musician of some stature, Luther had strong convictions about the value of music in worship and particularly that the congregation should participate in the service, including hymn singing.

*Chorale.* The most important musical contribution of the Lutheran Reformation was a new body of religious song called *chorale.* These hymns were intended primarily for congregational singing. There were four sources of chorale tunes: (1) plainsong melodies modified by metrical settings, and texts substituting German words for Latin, (2) nonliturgical German religious songs existing before the Reformation, (3) secular tunes with new religious texts added, a process known as *contrafactum,* and (4) newly composed hymns.

Chorales at first were monophonic, then they were set in simple four-part harmony with the chorale melody uppermost, and, finally, chorales were used in more elaborate contrapuntal settings for performance by chorus. Contrapuntal arrangements of chorales to be played on the organ were called *chorale preludes.*

*Composers.* The principal composers of Lutheran chorales and polyphonic settings were Sixtus Dietrich (c. 1490–1548), Johann Walter (1496–1570) who was Luther's musical collaborator, Thomas Stolzer (c. 1480–1526), Johannes Eccard (1553–1611), Hans Leo Hassler, and Michael Praetorius (1571–1621).

**France.** Music played a less significant role in Protestant movements in Switzerland under Zwingli and in France under Calvin, neither of whom was favorably disposed toward music in worship. The Huguenot movement, however, produced an important literature of psalms set to music.

*Psalms.* Biblical psalms were translated into French verse by Clément Marot (c. 1496–1544) and Théodore de Bèze (1519–1605), and set to melodies by Louis Bourgeois (c. 1510–c. 1561). They were intended for unison singing by the congregation and for use in the home. Also, four-part harmonizations as well as more elaborate contrapuntal arrangements were made.

*Composers.* The principal composers of Psalter music were Louis Bourgeois, Claude Goudimel (c. 1505–72), Claude Le Jeune (c. 1528–1600), and, in Holland, Jan Pieterszoon Sweelinck (1562–1621).

**England.** The rise of Protestantism in England was political rather than theological. Henry VIII officially broke with the Roman Church in 1534.

*Forms.* The English counterpart of the Catholic Mass was called the *Service,* the texts of which were set polyphonically. Anglican chant was derived mostly from Catholic plainsong. English texts were substituted for Latin, and the melodies were given metrical organization. In addition to Services, there were two Protestant forms of polyphony: (1) the *cathedral anthem* (or *full anthem*), which was like the Catholic motet but with English text, and (2) a later form, the *verse anthem,* which alternated solo and choral sections and used organ or string accompaniments.

Psalm singing was commonly practiced in England, too. The most important Psalter in England was composed by Thomas Sternhold (d. 1549) and John Hopkins (d. 1570). The 1612 Psalter by Henry Ainsworth (1571–c. 1622) was the one brought to the New World by the Pilgrims in 1620.

*Composers.* The principal composers of Anglican music were Tye, Tallis, and Byrd, all of whom also wrote Catholic music, and Orlando Gibbons (1583–1625), who composed both types of Protestant anthems.

### Secular Music

The current of renaissance secular polyphonic music, which began in the 15th century, continued its course into wider geographical areas, and became more diversified in form and style in an ever-expanding literature that flowed without interruption well into the 17th century.

**General Considerations.** (1) As in the 14th century, secular music again rivaled sacred music, largely because of the widespread renaissance spirit of secularization and also because poetry was flourishing. (2) The rise of national schools was even more pronounced in secular than in sacred music, although the influence of Netherlands composers was still strong. (3) Secular music flourished in all European courts under the patronage of nobility. (4) It should be remembered that renaissance secular music everywhere was intended as entertainment for amateur performers rather than as concert music. (5) It was composed and performed as chamber music for a few participants rather than for large choral ensembles.

**Italian Music.** Secular music which dominated the Italian Ars

Nova was not again significant until the 16th century, when Italian forms and styles influenced those of other countries.

*Forms.* In the late 15th century, a number of popular vocal forms, referred to collectively as *vocal canzoni,* included the *frottola* in northern Italy, the *villanella* in southern Italy, *carnival songs (canti carnascialeschi)* and *strambotti.* These unsophisticated forms were usually in four parts, strongly metrical, with dance-like rhythms, and predominantly chordal. They were the forerunners of the 16th-century Italian madrigal (unrelated to the 14th-century madrigal). As the Italian madrigal developed during the 16th century and into the 17th century, it became more polished, more contrapuntally elaborate, and more expressive. The use of musical devices pictorially descriptive of words or ideas in the text, called *madrigalism,* was characteristic. The late renaissance madrigal exploited striking chromatic effects in chordal passages.

A special class of madrigals called *madrigali spirituali* were nonliturgical compositions based on religious texts.

A type of madrigal called *balletto* was developed briefly in the later part of the century. It featured dance-like rhythms and contained refrains using nonsense syllables such as "fa-la-la."

A few madrigal cycles called *madrigal comedies* were composed at the end of the century. They were groups of madrigals based on pastoral subjects, loose plots, or humorous dialogues. *L'Amfiparnasso* by Orazio Vecchi (1550–1605) is the most famous of these. *Il Trionfo di Dori* is an important collection of madrigals by different composers.

*Composers.* Composers of canzoni and madrigals in the first half of the century were Philippe Verdelot (c. 1480–1540), Costanzo Festa (c. 1490–1545), Adrian Willaert, and Jacob Arcadelt (c. 1505–68). Late 16th- and early 17th-century composers were Cipriano de Rore (1516–65), Orlando di Lasso, Philippe de Monte, Giaches de Wert (or Jakob van Wert, 1535–96), Luca Marenzio (1553–99), Giovanni Gastoldi (c. 1555–1622), and Baldassare Donati (d. 1603), noted for balletti; Don Carlo Gesualdo (c. 1560–1613), famous for chromatic madrigals; and Claudio Monteverdi (1567–1643), whose madrigals represent the culmination of that form. It should be noted that some of the above composers were Netherlanders who were also important in

Catholic music and in secular music of other countries.

**French Music.** Although French secular music was somewhat influenced by Italian models, it retained a distinctly Gallic flavor. The high quality of French renaissance poetry (Ronsard and Baïf were among the gifted poets) contributed to the excellence of the music.

*Forms.* The polyphonic chanson, first developed by Netherlands composers, and the solo chanson with contrapuntal accompaniment continued in favor. Some chansons were in chordal style; others employed more elegant counterpoint with imitation. The *chanson rimée* employed regular metric rhythms. The *chanson mesurée*, a late 16th-century type, employed quantitative rhythms in which stressed syllables were given twice the note values of unstressed syllables, resulting in frequently shifting meters. A characteristic of many chansons, especially those using imitative counterpoint, was a repeated-note motive at the beginning of the initial theme (see Example 18 on page 65).

*Composers.* Principal names are Clément Jannequin (c. 1485–1560), noted for his descriptive *portraiture chansons,* Nicholas Gombert (c. 1490–1556), Claude de Sermisy (c. 1490–1562), Pierre Certon (c. 1510–72), Claude Le Jeune, Thomas Crécquillon (d. 1557), Orlando di Lasso, Claude Goudimel, Guillaume Costeley (c. 1531–1606), and Jacques Mauduit (1557–1627).

**English Music.** Secular music in Elizabethan England flourished somewhat later than on the Continent and continued to develop to nearly the middle of the 17th century.

*Forms.* The *English madrigal* received its initial impetus from Italy. In 1588 a collection of Italian madrigals with English translations was published in London. English madrigals usually employed a five-voice texture set to texts on pastoral and amorous subjects. Like French chansons, they were mostly in a light and gay style. Like Italian madrigals, they employed expressive devices (madrigalism).

A strophic form of madrigal called *ballett,* derived from the Italian balletto, used "fa-la-la" refrains in lively contrapuntal style alternating with chordal style for the stanzas.

The terms *canzonet* and *ayre,* which appear among English madrigal compositions, do not constitute types clearly distinct from the madrigal proper. In the late 16th and early 17th centuries, the *lute ayre* was much in vogue; it was a solo song with a contrapuntal lute accompaniment.

The most famous collection of English madrigals, entitled *The Triumphs of Oriana,* was patterned after the Italian *Il Trionfo di Dori.* Each madrigal concludes with the words "Long live fair Oriana," a reference to Queen Elizabeth I, to whom the collection was dedicated. It represents the peak of English madrigal composition by the most illustrious composers of the period.

*Composers.* The English madrigal school is represented by these composers: Thomas Morley (c. 1557–1603), who wrote madrigals, canzonets, and balletts, William Byrd, John Wilbye (c. 1574–1638), Thomas Weelkes (c. 1575–1623), John Ward (d. c. 1640), John Bennet (fl. 1600–1620), Thomas Bateson (c. 1570–1630), and Orlando Gibbons. Composers of lute ayres were Francis Pilkington (c. 1562–1638); Thomas Campion (1567–1620), and the most important of all, John Dowland (1562–1626).

**German Music.** German secular music in the 16th century was influenced by Netherland and Italian composers.

*Forms.* The *polyphonic lied* was the central type. For the most part it was a four-voice texture with imitative counterpoint. Popular songs were often the melodic basis.

Another popular form in the 15th and 16th centuries was the *quodlibet,* in which several different popular tunes and their texts were humorously and incongruously combined in a contrapuntal manner.

*Composers.* The composers of polyphonic lieder in the late 15th and early 16th centuries were Adam von Fulda (c. 1440–1506), Heinrich Finck (1445–1527), Heinrich Isaac, Paul Hofhaimer (1459–1537), and Ludwig Senfl. In the latter part of the 16th and early 17th centuries, the composers were Orlando di Lasso, Johannes Eccard, Hans Leo Hassler, and Melchior Franck (c. 1573–1639).

**Spanish Music.** Little is known about indigenous Spanish secular music before the late 15th century. Burgundian and Flemish composers were probably well known in Spain.

*Forms.* The principal Spanish form was the *villancico,* the counterpart of the Italian frottola (see p. 56). It was a four-part composition, predominantly in chordal style, and with a regular metric construction. It was based on a three-stanza poem, musically structured according to the formula *A B B A* in which the first stanza (*A*), called *estribillo,* was followed by the second stanza in two couplets to the same music (*B*), called *copla* or *mudanza,* and it concluded with the last stanza, called *vuelta,* sung to the same music as the first stanza. Villancicos may have been performed as solo songs with instruments playing the lower parts. The earliest literature of solo songs with *vihuela* (Spanish lute) accompaniments flourished in Spain during the 16th century.

*Composers.* The principal composer of villancicos was Juan del Encina (1468–1529). Some of his music is contained in a collection entitled *Cancionero del Palacio.* The leading composer of Spanish lute songs was Luis Milán (c. 1500–after 1561).

## Treatises

Among important treatises dealing with the theory and practice of music, the most important are *Practica Musicae* by Franchino Gaforio (1451–1522); *Musica Getutscht* by Sebastian Virdung, a treatise dealing mainly with instruments but important also because it discusses methods of transcribing vocal music to instrumental media; *Dodecachordon* by the Swiss theorist Henricus Glareanus (1488–1563), who, dealing with the subject of scales and modes, recommended the Ionian and Aeolian modes, thus reflecting the current trend toward major and minor tonalities; *Le Istituzioni Harmoniche* by Gioseffo Zarlino (1517–90); and *A Plaine and Easie Introduction to Practicall Musicke* by Thomas Morley, who treats a number of subjects relating to compositional techniques and performance.

**SCORES AND RECORDINGS**
 *Catholic Music*
  Mass: MM 24, HAM 106, 140, 143, 146b
  Motet: MM 23, 25, TEM 23, 28, HAM 109, 113, 114, 125, 127, 128, 139, 141, 144, 148, 149, 150, 152, 157, 164, 166
  Lauda: HAM 94
 *Reformation Music*
  Chorale and German motet: TEM 24, HAM 108, 110, 111, 167

Psalms: TEM 25, 26, HAM 126, 132
Cathedral anthem: TEM 27, HAM 169, 171
Verse anthem: HAM 151, 172

*Secular Music*

Chanson: MM 20, HAM 107, 138, 145, 147
Italian madrigal: MM 27, TEM 33, HAM 129, 130, 131, 142, 146, 155, 161
Frottola: TEM 20, HAM 95
Carnival song: HAM 96
Balletto (Italian): HAM 158
English madrigal: MM 28, HAM 163a
Ballett (English): HAM 159, 170
Lute ayre: TEM 34, HAM 162, 163b
Polyphonic lied: TEM 32, HAM 87, 93, 165, 168
Quodlibet: TEM 31, HAM 80
Villancico: TEM 19, HAM 97, 98
Spanish lute song: HAM 123

# CHAPTER 11

# Renaissance Instrumental Music

Although instrumental music in the Renaissance never matched the quantity or quality of vocal music, it is important because it reveals the rise of interest in instrumental media and the first realization of an independent instrumental idiom.

**General Considerations.** (1) With a few notable exceptions, instrumental music generally stayed within the limits of vocal idiom. (2) Improvisation played an important role in performance, especially in melodic ornamentation. (3) As in the Middle Ages, instruments were freely employed in the performance of vocal music, though they were not often specified. They were used to double or replace voice parts, and vocal compositions were even performed entirely by instruments. (4) Published transcriptions of vocal music for instrumental performance were numerous. (5) Some instrumental forms were directly derived from vocal forms; others were instrumentally conceived.

**Instrumental Style.** Where a distinctly instrumental style occurs in renaissance music it is manifested in these ways: (1) exceedingly rapid and long scale passages, (2) numerous wide skips, (3) melodic range wider than vocal limitations, (4) in lute and keyboard music, contrapuntal parts freely added or dropped out without rests indicated, (5) extensive ornamentation (coloration, embellishment, and figuration), and (6) a much freer treatment of dissonance. Most of these characteristics are illustrated in Example 17, an excerpt from a keyboard piece.

*Example 17. Instrumental style*

**Instruments.** There was a steady mechanical improvement in instruments during the Renaissance. The instruments in most common use fall mainly into three categories: strings, winds, and keyboard instruments. String and wind instruments were manufactured in families consisting of instruments ranging in size from the highest to lowest registers.

**Bowed Strings.** Renaissance viols, ancestors of the 17th-century violin family, were fretted instruments with six strings tuned in fourths with a third in the middle (A d g b e′ a′). They were used in various ensembles called *consorts,* consisting entirely of viols, or *mixed consorts,* with recorders and other instruments.

**Plucked Strings.** The lute was the most popular solo instrument. It had a pear-shaped body and angled neck. Lutes were fretted instruments with six strings tuned, like viols, in fourths with a third in the middle (G c f a d′ g′). Lute music was written in a special kind of notation called *tablature* which indicated the string and fret for a given note. (See Figure 6.) Lutes were used as solo instruments, accompanying instruments, and in some ensemble music.

In Spain, the guitar-like *vihuela* was the principal plucked-string instrument.

**Wind Instruments.** The most important renaissance wind instrument was the recorder, an end-blown wooden flute. Recorders, made in all sizes from treble to bass, were used in various kinds of ensemble music. The *shawm* and *cromorn* were double-reed woodwinds. *Cornets,* made of wood or ivory, were soft-toned instruments. Various kinds of trumpets and trombones were in use, but they were limited to the natural tones of the harmonic series. Such instruments were confined to fanfares or to outdoor festival music for large ensembles.

**Keyboard Instruments.** Large church organs were built in the

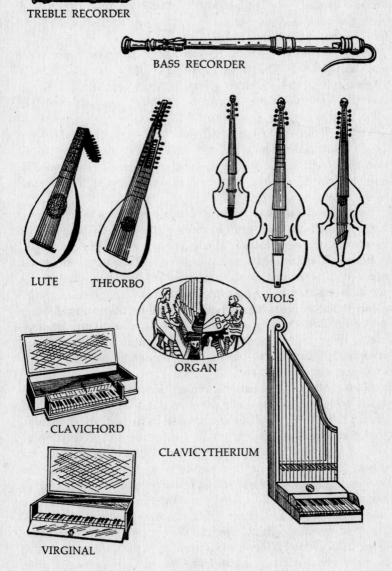

TREBLE RECORDER

BASS RECORDER

LUTE THEORBO

VIOLS

ORGAN

CLAVICHORD

CLAVICYTHERIUM

VIRGINAL

Figure 3
*Some instruments of the Renaissance*

Renaissance, but only in Germany did they have pedalboards. *Positive organs* (also called *regals*) had been in common use since the Middle Ages, but the portative organ disappeared before the end of the 15th century.

String keyboard instruments were of two types: *clavichord* and *harpsichord*. The latter were also designated as *spinet*, *virginal* (English), *clavecin* (French), *clavicembalo* (Italian), and *Klavier* or *Clavier* (German terms which also included the clavichord).

A considerable solo literature was composed for all the keyboard instruments. The organ was also used to accompany vocal polyphony but not in instrumental ensembles. The harpsichord and clavichord were less often used as accompanying instruments or in ensembles.

*Ensembles.* Renaissance instrumental ensembles were almost entirely small chamber groups, rarely orchestras. Specific instrumentation of ensembles was almost never indicated in the scores.

**Forms.** The fact that renaissance composers were not much concerned with distinctions between instrumental and vocal media is attested to by inscriptions such as "per cantar e sonar" (for singing and playing) which appeared on title pages. A large portion of 16th-century instrumental music consisted of arrangements of sacred and secular vocal compositions, but originally composed instrumental pieces were numerous and some new instrumental forms evolved.

*Dance Music.* The earliest extant dance music was largely intended to accompany social dancing, but during the second half of the 16th century stylized dance music was favored. Generally, dance music had strong rhythm, and structures consisting of several repeated sections. Renaissance dances were often composed in pairs or groups of three. In dance pairs, the first dance was in slow tempo, the second in fast tempo and with change of meter. Both dances often used the same tune. The most popular dance pair was the *pavane* (also *padovano, paduana*) in slow duple time and *gaillarde* in fast triple time. An Italian dance pair was the *ronde* and *saltarello*. German dance pairs were designated as *Tanz und Nachtanz* or else *Der Prinzen Tanz-Proportz*. Other dances were *passamezzo, basse-danse, branle* (also *bransle*) and, toward the close of the century, *allemande* (*alman*) and *courante* (*corrento*).

Dance music was composed for various ensembles, lute, and harpsichord.

**Cantus Firmus Forms.** Compositions based on plainsong, chorale, or secular song were composed for organ, harpsichord, and sometimes ensembles of viols. They had some liturgical function as *verses* or *versets* played by the organist between verses of a hymn sung by the congregation or choir. Most cantus firmus music was conservatively styled in vocal idiom.

**Fugal Forms.** In this category belong a number of forms which made prominent use of contrapuntal imitation. Organ transcriptions of motets were common. Original organ pieces composed in motet style were called *ricercare*. Such pieces were also composed for lute and instrumental ensembles. A fugal form derived from the French polyphonic chanson was called *canzona* (or *canzona francese*). Canzonas, composed for instrumental ensembles (*canzona da sonar*), harpsichord, or organ (*canzona d'organo*), were more lively in rhythm and tempo than the ricercare, and they employed the characteristic repeated-note motives of the chanson (see Example 18).

*Example 18. Canzona style*

Other fugal forms were the *fantasia* (also *fantasy, fancy*) and *capriccio*.

**Improvisational Forms.** Instrumental types which made use of various materials conveying a sense of improvisation were the *prelude* (also *praeludium, praeambulum*). Such pieces were composed for lute or one of the keyboard instruments.

**Variation Forms.** Forms based on the principle of variation are the oldest to have a continuous history to the present. They were first developed by the Spanish vihuelists and later in the 16th century by the English virginalists. It was perhaps in variations that composers first fully explored instrumental idioms. Variations were constructed in several different ways. (1) *Cantus firmus variations* were based on a given melody restated a number of times with little or no change, but with each statement the melody was accompanied by different counterpoint and in a different voice. (2) The *theme and variations* form was based on a popular tune which itself was modified with each restatement. (3) English *hexachord variations* used as a theme the first six notes of a scale. Variations of this type were usually entitled *Ut re mi fa sol la* and were common in virginal music. (4) A variations form called *ground* was based on a short theme of four to eight measures in the bass with continuous and changing counterpoint above.

**Schools and Composers.** As a general rule, most composers of renaissance instrumental music wrote little vocal music, and they usually specialized in one medium. Notable exceptions were some of the English virginal composers and some of the Venetian composers late in the century.

*Germany.* A long line of German organ composers began with Conrad Paumann (c. 1410–73), whose *Fundamentum Organisandi* contained two-part organ pieces. Other organ composers were Hans Buchner (1483–1538), Hans Kotter (c. 1485–1541), Leonhard Kleber (c. 1490–1556), Paul Hofhaimer, and Arnold Schlick (c. 1460–after 1527).

Lute composers were Hans Judenkünig (c. 1460–1526), Hans Gerle (d. 1570), and Hans Neusiedler (also Newsidler, c. 1508–63).

Composers of instrumental ensemble music were Nicolaus Ammerbach (c. 1530–97), Valentin Hausmann (late 16th century), and Melchior Franck.

*Spain.* The leading Spanish vihuela composer was Luis Milán. His contemporaries were Luis de Narvaez, Enriquez de Valderrábano, and Miguel de Fuenllana. Antonio Cabezón (1510–66) was the outstanding composer of Spanish organ music.

*Italy.* Francesco Spinaccino and Ambrosio Dalza were early 16th-century lute composers. More important was the organ music of Claudio Merulo (1533–1604), Cirolamo Cavazzoni (b. c. 1520), Annibale Padovano (b. c. 1527), Andrea and Giovanni Gabrieli, and Jean de Macque (c. 1550–1614). Composers of instrumental ensemble music were Florentio Maschera (1540–84) and the two Gabrielis.

*France.* The first French music printer, Pierre Attaingnant (d. c. 1550), published numerous collections of organ, lute, and clavecin music by unnamed composers. Jean Titelouze (1563–1633) composed cantus-firmus organ pieces based on plainsong.

*England.* The English virginal school includes the names of Hugh Aston (c. 1480–c. 1522), Giles Farnaby (c. 1560–1640), William Byrd, John Bull (c. 1562–1628), and Orlando Gibbons. The most important among several collections of virginal music is *The Fitzwilliam Virginal Book.*

Organ music, less important in England, is represented by John Redford (1485–1545) and John Bull in the early 17th century. English lute music was composed mainly by John Dowland, Francis Pilkington, and Thomas Campion. Orlando Gibbons also composed fantasias for viols.

## SCORES AND RECORDINGS

Examples of instrumental music are listed here according to form rather than by schools or media. Medium is indicated by the symbols *l* (lute), *h* (harpsichord), *o* (organ) *v* (viols), and *e* (ensemble).

Dance: MM 22 (*l*), TEM 30 (*h*), 35 (*e*), HAM 83 (*e*), 102 (*h*), 103 (*h*), 104 (*h*), 105 (*l*), 137 (*e*), 154 (*e*), 167b (*e*), 179 (*h*)

Cantus firmus: TEM 24 (*o*), 36 (*e*), HAM 100 (*o*), 117 (*o*), 120 (*o*), 133 (*o*), 176 (*v*), 180 (*o*)

Canzona: MM 21 (*h*), 26 (*o*), HAM 88 (*e*), 118 (*o*), 136 (*e*), 175 (*e*)

Fantasia: HAM 121 (*l*), 181 (*o*)

Ricercare: HAM 99 (*l*), 115 (*e*), 116 (*o*), 119 (*v*), 173 (*e*)

Toccata: TEM 29 (*o*), HAM 153 (*o*), 174 (*o*)

Prelude: HAM 84 (*o*), 135 (*o*), 178 (*h*)

Variations: MM 29 (*h*); HAM 122 (*l*), 124 (*l*) 134 (*o*), 154b (*h*), 177 (*h*), 179 (*h*)

Transcriptions of vocal music: MM 20–21 (*h*), TEM 21 (*l*); HAM 81b (*o*), 160 (*h, l*)

# CHAPTER 12

# Musical Notation

The history of musical notation is an evolution toward accurate symbolic representation of two musical factors: pitch and duration of tone. Progress was generally slow and, until the Renaissance, methods and styles of writing music varied considerably from one locality to another. Modern notation dates from the early 17th century. Prior to 1600, various other systems had been used. The principal systems of Western notation were neumatic, modal, and mensural notation.

## Neumatic Notation

Although numerous attempts at notation were made in pre-Christian times and during most of the first millennium of the Christian era, they were largely unsuccessful. The history of Western notation began near the end of the 9th century.

**Neumes.** Plainsong notation was first recorded by signs called *neumes.* They originated as chironomic inflection symbols: acute ( ╱ ), grave ( ╲ ), and circumflex ( ∧ ). Placed above words of a text, neumes served merely as reminders of the general upward or downward direction of a melody already known. The number of neumatic note forms increased to more than a dozen signs.

**Diastematic Notation.** At first, neumes were written only above some of the words of a text and *in campo aperto* ("in the open field" without any indication of relative pitch). By the early 10th century, neumes were written in relatively high or low positions, a practice known as *diastematic* or *heighted* neumes (see Figure 4). These provided a more accurate guide to melodic contours, but they still did not indicate exact pitch, intervals, or duration of notes.

Figure 4
*Diastematic notation*

St. Gall, *Cantarorium* (late 9th century), Cod. 359, fol. 125. Reproduced from Carl Parrish, *The Notation of Medieval Music*, Plate II. Reprinted by permission from W. W. Norton.

**Figure 5**
*One-line neumatic notation*

Reproduced from Homer Ulrich and Paul Pisk, *A History of Music and Musical Style*, p. 36. Reprinted by permission from Harcourt, Brace & World.

**Staff Notation.** The first important step toward indicating exact pitch, initiated near the end of the 10th century, was the introduction of a horizontal line representing the tone F, above or below which neumes were written (see Figure 5). This was the origin

### III. — On Solemn Feasts. 2.
(Kyrie Deus sempiterne)

Figure 6
*Modern plainsong notation*

"Kyrie Deus Sempiterne," reproduced from *Plain Song for Schools*, p. 12.
Reprinted by permission from J. Cary & Co., London.

of the *staff*. Soon thereafter, two-line staves in color were used to indicate the tones F (upper line, red) and C (lower line, green or yellow). By the 11th century four-line staves were described by Guido d'Arezzo. This is the staff used in modern Georgian notation (see Figure 6). More and more lines were added, up to eleven or more, then separated into two staves by eliminating the middle-C line. Eventually, by about the 13th century, five-line staves were favored.

**Clef Signs.** Medieval scribes used the letters C, F, and G placed on one of the staff lines to indicate the pitch of that line and, by inference, the pitches of all the other lines. Modern clefs are derived from these same letters in old script.

## Modal Notation

Notation from the end of the 12th century to about the middle of the 13th century is referred to as *modal notation* because it was based on the rhythmic modes (see page 29). Although it achieved some degree of mensurality indicating relative duration of notes, considerable ambiguity existed because the duration of a note was affected both by its shape and its context in the pattern of the mode.

**Notes.** Modal notation is also called *square notation* because of its note shapes as opposed to the various forms used in neumatic notation. Three types of notes were the *long* (or *longa* ¶ ), the *breve* (or *brevis* ▪ ), and *semibreve* (or *semibrevis* ♦ ). These notes were used singly and in groups called *ligatures* (see Example 19).

*Example 19. Ligatures*

**Perfection.** Modal notation was based on a concept of triple division called *perfection,* in which a note of one denomination was equal to three of the next smaller denomination.

**Music in Modal Notation.** Music written in modal notation included some of the troubadour and trouvère songs, clausulae, organa, conductus, and some of the earliest motets. Plainsong and some secular monophonic songs continued to be written in the older neumatic notation.

## Mensural Notation

Notation in use from the second half of the 13th century to the end of the 16th century is referred to as *mensural notation* (measured notation). The 13th century witnessed the transition from modal to mensural notation. The 13th and 14th centuries were periods of rapid and often complex developments. Problems and uncertainties still existed, but mensural notation finally achieved a high degree of accuracy in representing relative duration.

**Franconian Notation.** Notation in the second half of the 13th century is called *Franconian notation* after Franco of Cologne who described the current system in his *Ars Cantus Mensurabilis* around 1260. The Franconian system used the same kinds of black notes as in modal notation (long, breve, and semibreve). The breve became the basic time unit and its division was still predominantly perfect (triple). Around 1280, Petrus de Cruce was using more than three semibreves to a breve.

**Choirbooks.** Until about 1230 polyphonic music was notated in *score* in which the various parts were arranged one above the other on one or more staves. This plan was abandoned in favor of *choirbook* arrangement. The two upper parts of a three-voice composition were placed either on opposite pages or else in two columns on a single page, and the tenor part was notated on one continuous staff across the bottom of the page (see Figure 7). The reason for this change was probably that the textless tenor part, which had fewer notes, left too much valuable parchment space in the score form, whereas in the choirbook arrangement it could be greatly condensed. Choirbooks remained in use until about the middle of the 16th century.

**Ars Nova Notation.** French and Italian composers in the 14th century developed mensural notation still further and established the basic principles which remained in effect throughout the Renaissance.

**Characteristics.** In his treatise entitled *Ars Nova* (c. 1325), Philippe de Vitry recognized duple and triple meter as being equally important. The late 14th century used a system of great complexity, referred to as *mannered notation*. The long was less often used, and the *minim* ( ♩ ) and *semiminim* ( ♪ ) were added. Notes colored red in the manuscripts were used to indicate

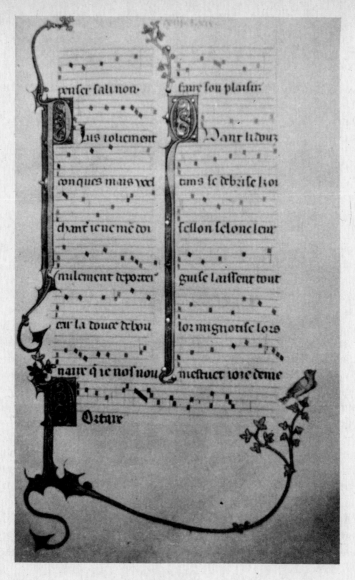

**Figure 7**
*Franconian notation and choirbook arrangement*

Three-voice motet: "Plus joliement/Quant le douz/Portare." Reproduced from *Chansonnier de Montpellier,* Ms. H 196. Reprinted by permission from Le Conservateur en Chef, Bibliothèque Universitaire, Section de Médecine, Montpellier, France.

imperfection (duple division) and also to indicate a change of proportion as, for example, three red notes equal to two black notes of the same denomination.

*Mode, Time, and Prolation.* In the 14th-century system each note was subject either to duple or triple division. The relation of long to breve was called *mode;* the relation of breve to semibreve was called *time;* and the relation of semibreve to minim was called *prolation.* A long was usually equal to two breves (*imperfect mode*). A breve could equal two semibreves (*imperfect time*) or three semibreves (*perfect time*). A semibreve could equal two minims (*minor prolation*) or three minims (*major prolation*). These five relationships are represented in Example 20, a table of note values.

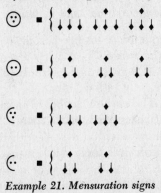

Mode:    imperfect

Time:    { perfect / imperfect }

Prolation:    { major / minor }

*Example 20. Note values in mode, time, and prolation*

*Mensuration Signs.* Time and prolation were represented by two signs each, one for triple and one for duple division. Perfect time was represented by a full circle ( ○ ), imperfect time by a half-circle ( ⊂ ). Major prolation was represented by three dots, minor prolation by two dots. Thus, time and prolation were combined in four ways (see Example 21).

*Example 21. Mensuration signs*

An additional sign, a half circle with a vertical line drawn through the center ( ¢ ), indicated that notes were to get half the normal value. This was called *alla breve*. The sign and the term are both still used today, as is also the C for $\frac{4}{4}$ meter.

**Dots.** In addition to dots used for prolation in mensuration signs, they were also used in two other ways: (1) a dot (called *punctus*) following a note could indicate the separation of basic note units (called *point of division*) comparable to the modern bar line; or (2) it could indicate the addition of half the note's value (called *point of addition*), the same as in use today.

**Renaissance Notation.** From about the middle of the 15th century to the end of the 16th century, mensural notation was ultimately standardized in what is called *classical mensural notation*. The complexities of *Ars Nova* notation largely disappeared. White breves, semibreves, and minims ( ⊟ ◇ ↓ ) replaced the former black notes. The semiminim had a new form ( ↓ ), and the fusa ( ↓ ) was added. Mensuration signs were the same as before except that a single dot ( ⊙ or ⊝ ) now indicated major prolation, and no dot ( ○ or ⊂ ) meant minor prolation. Sixteenth-century notation is shown in Figure 8.

**Partbooks.** In the second half of the 16th century, *partbooks* replaced choirbooks. In the newer plan, single parts for a number of different compositions were bound together in one volume. Thus, four-part music would require four separate books, one each for soprano, alto, tenor, and bass parts. The disadvantage of this system is obvious, and ultimately in the 17th century, part music came once again to be written in score.

## Keyboard and Lute Notation

The history of notation thus far has dealt exclusively with vocal music. With the exception of early Greek notation, there was no special notation for instrumental music or intended instrumental parts until the early 14th century.

**Organ Tablature.** The earliest keyboard music is preserved in *The Robertsbridge Codex* (early 14th century) which contains two-part organ pieces written on a staff with the upper part in notes and the lower part in letters. This system, commonly called *German organ tablature*, was the means of writing organ compositions until the end of the 16th century.

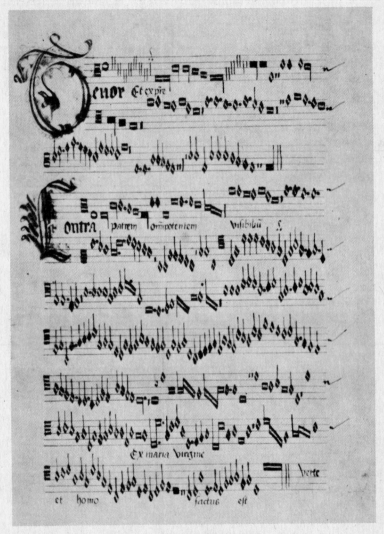

### Figure 8
*Classical mensural notation*

Tenor and contratenor parts of *Missa l'Homme Armé*, "Patrem Omni-potentum," Faugues. Biblioteca Apostolico-Vaticana, Cappella Sistina 14, fol. 143ʳ. (Retouched, reproduced by permission of The Institute of Medieval Music).

*Lute Tablature.* Renaissance composers of lute music devised a special kind of notation called *lute tablature*. Instead of writing notes or letters on a staff they used six parallel horizontal lines which represented the six strings of a lute. Since the lute was a fretted instrument, letters or numerals placed on a line indicated where the finger stopped the string. Numerals were used in Spanish and Italian tablatures, letters in French, English, and most German tablatures. The cipher (0) in numeral tablature and the letter *a* in alphabet tablature indicated the open string to be played. Hence, the number 2 or the letter *c* on a line indicated the second half-step above the open string. Rhythmic signs were placed above the tablature lines (see Figure 9). Similar tablatures were occasionally used also for viols.

**Harpsichord Notation.** Music for harpsichord was notated in keyboard score, usually on two five-line staves, the same as it is today.

## Unquiet Thoughts

Figure 9

*English lute tablature and transcription*

Dowland, "Unquiet Thoughts." Reprinted from *English Lute-Song Writers*, vol. 1, p. 2, by permission from Stainer & Bell, London.

# IV

*The*

*Baroque*

*(1600—1750)*

# CHAPTER 13

# General Considerations

The century and a half from the end of the 16th century to the middle of the 18th century is known as the baroque era. The aesthetic ideal of the Baroque permeated virtually all aspects of European culture, although the Baroque, as did the Renaissance, began in Italy. Drama, painting, architecture, and music were characterized by grandiose concepts, magnificent effects, contrasts, ornate design, and an overall theatrical quality.

**Historical Background.** Important historical events of the 17th century were the Thirty Years' War in Germany (1618–48), the reign of Louis XIV of France from 1643 to 1715, the English Civil War (1642–49), the Commonwealth and Protectorate (1649–60), and the Restoration (1660). It was a time of worldwide colonization. Illustrious names in science were Newton, Harvey, Galileo, Bacon, Kepler, and Leibnitz. The foremost philosophers were Locke, Descartes, Pascal, and Spinoza. Leading artists of the period were the Dutch painters Rembrandt, Reubens, and Van Dyck, the English Hogarth, and, of the Spanish school, El Greco and Velásquez. English literature was represented by Milton, Dryden, Defoe, Addison, Swift, Pope, and Samuel Johnson; French literature, by Corneille, Racine, and Molière.

**General Musical Characteristics.** Although changes in style and form took place continuously throughout the period, certain traits generally set baroque music apart from that of other periods.

*Stile Concertato.* A distinctly baroque characteristic was called *concertato style* (*stile concertato*). It was a concept in which different media were in opposition to one another, either simultaneously or in alternation: vocal against instrumental, and solo against ensemble.

**Basso Continuo.** The lowest part in most baroque ensemble music was the *basso continuo* or *thoroughbass*. Functioning both as melodic and harmonic bass, it was played by the combination of two kinds of instruments: (1) one or more melody instruments (viola da gamba, cello, or bassoon) and (2) a keyboard instrument (organ or harpsichord) or lute. The basso continuo part was written in the bass clef with numerals and accidentals below the notes, a musical shorthand known as *figured bass*. It was the duty of the keyboard or lute performer to fill in the harmony indicated by the numerals, a procedure called *realizing* the figured bass. Numerals indicated the characteristic interval above the bass note. For instance, a 6 indicated a first inversion chord, a 7 designated a seventh chord. Absence of a numeral meant a chord in root position. A sharp, flat, or natural sign by itself indicated the corresponding alteration of the third of the chord. A line through a numeral indicated raising the upper note of that interval. Some of these signs are illustrated in Example 22, a figured bass, along with its harmonic realization.

*Example 22. Figured bass and realization*

**Harmony.** The figured bass reflected a new harmonic concept in music, replacing the older intervallic basis of renaissance practice. Chords and their inversions, however, were not fully recognized until the late Baroque in Rameau's *Traité de* *l'Harmonie* (1722). Authentic cadences (V I) replaced the older modal cadences. Chromaticism played a more prominent role. Systematic *modulation* (a harmonic progression which begins in one key and ends in another) became commonplace. Seventh chords were introduced without preparation. Treatment of dissonance was freer and no longer restricted to passing tones, suspensions, and so on, although they continued to be used extensively.

**Tonality.** The modern concept of major and minor tonalities finally replaced modality, although the latter was in evidence to a slight extent through the 17th century. Compositions came to indicate keys in their titles (Sonata in D Minor, Mass in B Minor, Suite in A Major), and they conveyed a stronger sense of tonal center than before.

**Texture.** Baroque texture was still predominantly contrapuntal, but there was a new emphasis on homophony in certain types of music where a single melodic line was supported by harmonic material. Counterpoint was harmonically oriented, and it reached new heights of technical mastery in the hands of Bach and others. Another aspect of baroque texture was the relative prominence of the bass.

**Tempo and Dynamics.** For the first time in music history composers began to indicate tempo (e.g., adagio, allegro) and dynamics (e.g., forte, piano), reflecting their concern with more adequate expression of the "affections" (emotional content or mood). However, the use of tempo and dynamics indications was by no means universal.

**Improvisation.** Although not entirely a new discipline, improvisation played a more important part in performance than at any other time in the history of music. Musicians were highly trained in the art of improvising melodic ornaments, variations on a theme, cadenzas, and the realization of figured basses with elaborate contrapuntal material.

**New Forms.** New multimovement vocal forms developed in the Baroque were *opera, cantata,* and *oratorio.* New multimovement instrumental forms were the *sonata, suite,* and *concerto.* The principal contrapuntal form to emerge in the Baroque was the *fugue,* composed in all instrumental and choral media.

**Dual Style.** Renaissance techniques in vocal polyphony

flourished well into the 17th century, coexisting with radically new Italian innovations at the beginning of the century. Well aware of this dual style, composers referred to the continuing renaissance technique as "the old style" (*stile antico*) or "the first practice" (*prima prattica*) and, correspondingly, to the new kind of music as "the modern style" (*stile moderno*) or "the second practice" (*seconda prattica*).

**Nuove Musiche.** The beginning of the 17th century saw a conscious revolt against renaissance polyphony, which the protagonists wanted to replace with entirely new techniques. The innovations, instigated by a group of Florentine noblemen called the *Camerata*, included figured bass, *monody* (accompanied solo song), *recitative*, and a new concept of drama with music called *opera*.

Among a number of historically important works of the early 17th century was a collection of monodies with figured bass accompaniment composed by Giulo Caccini (c. 1546–1618) entitled *Le Nuove Musiche* (1602). From this title early 17th century music practice took its name.

**Important Composers.** Further evidence of the growth of musical art is to be seen in the increase in the number of first-rank composers. The most outstanding among these are listed here.

**Italy.** Claudio Monteverdi (1567–1643), a master of both the first and second "practices," wrote madrigals and operas. Giacomo Carissimi (1605–74) was a master of oratorio. Alessandro Scarlatti (1660–1725) composed operas, secular cantatas, and church music. His son, Domenico Scarlatti (1685–1757) was noted for harpsichord sonatas. Arcangelo Corelli (1653–1713) and Antonio Vivaldi (c. 1669–1741) were masters of chamber and orchestral music.

**France.** Jean Baptiste Lully (c. 1632–87) wrote operas and ballets. François Couperin (1668–1733) worked principally in the area of clavecin music. The culminating figure in French baroque music was Jean Philippe Rameau (1683–1764), who wrote operas, keyboard music, and was the most important theorist of the period.

**England.** The one great English composer of the middle Baroque was Henry Purcell (1658–95) who composed vocal and instrumental music in most of the forms of his time. George

Frideric Handel (1685–1759), though German by birth and Italian by training, spent most of his creative life in London, where he wrote and produced operas and oratorios as well as a quantity of instrumental music in various media. He is considered one of the great culminating figures of baroque music.

*Germany.* Johann Hermann Schein (1586–1630) and Samuel Scheidt (1587–1654) were early baroque composers of keyboard music; Johann Jacob Froberger (1616–67) was the leading German composer of middle baroque keyboard music. Michael Praetorius (1571–1621) composed choral music in the dual styles. Heinrich Schütz (1585–1672) was the leading German composer of middle baroque church music. Dietrich Buxtehude (1637–1707) and Johann Pachelbel (1653–1706) were Bach's immediate predecessors in organ and church music. One of the most prolific and versatile composers of the late Baroque was Georg Philipp Telemann (1681–1767), who composed cantatas, operas, chamber and orchestral music. Finally, the most venerated composer of late baroque music was Johann Sebastian Bach (1685–1750), who was the ultimate master of counterpoint and every baroque category of music except opera.

# CHAPTER 14

# Opera and Vocal Chamber Music

Opera was born at the turn of the 17th century as the central innovation of Italian *nuove musiche*. It soon influenced virtually all types of baroque music. Other secular vocal forms were solo songs and chamber cantatas.

**Forerunners of Opera.** The association of music and drama goes back to Antiquity. Greek tragedies employed choruses, and dialogue may have been sung. Medieval liturgical dramas, mystery plays, and miracle plays were at least partly sung. Renaissance plays made use of musical interludes between acts, called *intermezzi* or *intermedi*. Madrigal comedies of the late 16th century approached the idea of musical narrative and dialogue, though they were not intended for stage performance.

**Components of Opera.** Operas, like plays, are performed on a stage, and they include acting, scenery, costumes, properties, and lighting. The text of an opera is called a *libretto*. The musical components are: (1) solo song, in opera called *aria*, (2) ensembles of two or more solo voices, called *duet, trio,* and so on, (3) *recitative,* a declamatory style of singing dialogue, (4) *chorus,* (5) the *orchestra,* which accompanies singing and provides instrumental introductions and interludes (*ritornelli*), (6) the *overture,* the instrumental introduction to an opera, and (7) in some operas, formal dances called *ballet.*

## Italian Opera

The main stream in Italian opera was centered, more or less consecutively, around four Italian cities: Florence, Rome, Venice, and Naples.

**Florentine Opera.** In the last decade of the 16th century, a group of Florentine noblemen, the Camerata, sought to revive ancient Greek tragedy. Although as classical scholars they were aware of the function of music in drama, they also realized that polyphonic madrigal style was not suitable for dramatic expression. Consequently they initiated a new style of singing called *stile rappresentativo* (theater style) for their dramas, which became the earliest operas.

*Composers.* Probably the first opera (now lost) was written in 1597 by the Florentine poet Ottavio Rinuccini (1562–1621) with music composed by Jacopo Peri (1561–1633); both were members of the Camerata. The first extant opera was *Euridice,* libretto by Rinuccini and music jointly composed by Peri and Caccini in 1600 for the festivities in connection with the wedding of Henry IV of France and Maria de' Medici in Florence. In the following year, each composer published his own version of the opera.

The most important opera composer in the first half of the 17th century was Claudio Monteverdi, whose *Orfeo,* in 1607, assimilated the new techniques of the Camerata and achieved greater dramatic expression.

**Roman Opera.** For the next two decades little transpired in opera development until Rome became the center in the 1630s.

*Characteristics.* Roman opera was based more on religious subjects than on Greek mythology, and it made more use of choruses. Distinction between recitative and aria began to emerge. The prototype of comic opera were *intermezzi,* comic interludes between the acts.

*Composers.* The principal composers were Stefano Landi (c. 1590–1655), who composed *Saint Alexis* (*Santo Alessio*), and Luigi Rossi (1597–1653), whose principal opera was another *Orfeo.*

**Venetian Opera.** Shortly before the middle of the century, Venice assumed the leadership which it retained to the end of the century. The first public opera house, Teatro San Cassiano, was opened in Venice in 1637.

*Characteristics.* The principal characteristics of Venetian opera were: (1) more emphasis on formal arias, (2) the beginning of *bel canto* ("beautiful singing") style, and more attention to vocal elegance than to dramatic expression, (3) less use of chorus and orchestral music, (4) complex and improbable plots, (5) elaborate stage machinery, and (6) short fanfare-like instrumental introductions, the prototypes of the later overture.

*Composers.* The principal composers and operas of the Venetian school were Pier Francesco Cavalli (1602–76), who wrote *Giasone,* and Marc' Antonio Cesti (1623–69), whose most important opera was *Il Pomo d'Oro.* Monteverdi's last operas, produced in Venice, were *Il Ritorno d'Ulisse* and *L'Incoronazione di Poppea.* Later Venetian composers were Marc Antonio Sartorio (c. 1620–85) and Giovanni Legrenzi (1626–90).

**Neapolitan Opera.** A school of composers in Naples emerged in the second half of the century and dominated European opera in the 18th century.

*Characteristics.* In general, operas became more formalized and artificial from the dramatic standpoint. They consisted mainly of *da capo arias* (*A-B-A* sectional structure). Another type of aria introduced by the Neapolitans was the *siciliana* in slow tempo, $\frac{6}{8}$ meter, and usually in a minor key. Choruses were almost nonexistent, and the orchestra was relegated to a subordinate accompanying role. Less important than arias, recitatives were composed in two styles: (1) "dry recitative" (*recitativo secco*), which was a declamatory melody with sparse continuo accompaniment, and (2) "accompanied recitative" (*recitativo accompagnato,* also called *recitativo strumento*) which employed a more active orchestral accompaniment for especially dramatic passages of dialogue. Still another style of operatic song was the *arioso,* a compromise between recitative and aria. *Castrati* (male sopranos) reigned supreme as the opera stars of the day, and they were responsible for the excesses of showy virtuosity with improvised display of vocal gymnastics. The Italian overture, called *sinfonia,* was established as a formal plan in three sections: fast-slow-fast. The sinfonia was the forerunner of the later classical symphony.

*Composers.* The central figure of Neapolitan opera was Alessandro Scarlatti, who composed some 114 operas. Other composers were Alessandro Stradella (1642–82), Carlo Pallavicini (1630–88), Francesco Provenzale (1627–1704), Agostino Steffani (1654–1728), Nicola Porpora (1686–1768), Leonardo Vinci (1690–1730), Attilio Ariosti (1666–c. 1740), and Giovanni Bononcini

(1670–1747). Handel, in London, was the last composer of Neapolitan-style operas in the Baroque.

## French Opera and Ballet

France developed an indigenous opera to a greater extent than any other country outside Italy, but that development did not come until the second half of the 17th century.

**Characteristics.** French opera was strongly influenced by two flourishing national institutions: the court ballet and the dramas of Corneille, Racine, and Molière. As compared to Italian opera, the outstanding traits of French opera were: (1) use of ballet, (2) greater importance of the drama, (3) more use of the orchestra and instrumental music, (4) shorter and simpler dance-like airs, (5) careful attention to accentuation of the text, (6) more expressive and melodic recitative, (7) less emphasis on virtuosity, and (8) the French *ouverture* (overture), which became an important instrumental form in the Baroque. The ouverture consisted of two sections, each repeated: the first in slow tempo and dotted rhythm, the second in lively tempo and fugal texture. Later, the French overture included a third section in slow tempo, similar to the first.

**Ballet.** Court dances with costume and scenery, but without singing or spoken dialogue, were common in the Renaissance. The earliest extant ballet music was the *Ballet Comique de la Reine* in 1581. Royalty customarily took part in the performances of ballets which flourished in the court of Louis XIV at Versailles. Lully's *Ballet de la Nuit* was a court ballet. Lully and Molière collaborated to create a new form, the *comédie-ballet*, which was a combination of play and ballet. *Le Bourgeois Gentilhomme* was the most famous of these. Later, Lully introduced ballets into his operas, which he called *tragédies-lyriques* or *opéra-ballets*.

**Composers.** The first opera in the French language was called *Pastorale* and was written in 1659 by Abbé Pierre Perrin (c. 1620–75), librettist, and Robert Cambert (c. 1628–77). It marked the opening of the Royal Academy of Music in Paris.

Lully was the leading composer of French opera and ballet in the second half of the 17th century. In addition to his court ballets and comédie-ballets, his principal works (tragédies-lyriques) were *Cadmus et Hermione, Alceste, Amadis,* and *Armide.*

The principal operas by Rameau, who represents the culmination of French baroque opera, are *Hippolyte et Aricie* and *Castor et Pollux.*

## Opera in England

Indigenous serious opera never achieved the popular following in England that it did in Italy and France. Many Italian operas were performed in London. The principal types of theater music in England were the masque, incidental and entr'acte music, and ballad opera.

**Opera.** Two works represent virtually the entire repertory of serious English opera. One was *Venus and Adonis* by John Blow (1649–1708); the other was *Dido and Aeneas* by Purcell.

**Masque.** A kind of theatrical court entertainment called *masque* was in vogue in England in the 17th century. Masques, which were lavish productions performed privately for nobility, were plays based on mythological and allegorical subjects, and they included songs (called *ayres*), poetry reading, dances, choruses, instrumental pieces, and occasionally recitatives. A famous masque was *Comus* by poet John Milton with music by Henry Lawes (1596–1662).

**Incidental and Entr'acte Music.** A significant amount of *incidental music* was written to be performed during the action of plays, and *entr'acte music* for performance between scenes or acts. The latter consisted of instrumental pieces, called *act tunes* or *curtain tunes.* Examples of incidental music are Purcell's music for *The Fairy Queen* (after Shakespeare's *Midsummer Night's Dream*) and *King Arthur.* Entr'acte music is represented by Locke's *Instrumental Musick used in "The Tempest"* and Purcell's music for *Dioclesian.* Incidental and entr'acte music for some plays was so extensive that they approached true opera.

## Opera in Germany

A dearth of indigenous opera in Germany was due to the impact of Italian opera in that country and also the cultural disruption of the Thirty Years' War. Furthermore, there was little German libretto literature of quality.

Aside from an early opera by Schütz, *Daphne* (now lost), nearly all operatic activity in Germany consisted of Italian operas performed by Italian companies. Even German composers were for a while content to write operas in Italian style to Italian texts. *Costanza e Fortezza* by Johann Fux (1660–1741) was such an opera. Italian opera flourished in Vienna, Munich, and Dresden.

German opera, called *Singspiel,* began in Hamburg where an opera house opened in 1678 with *Adam und Eva* by Johann Theile (1646–1724). Other names connected with Hamburg opera were Reinhard Keiser (1674–1739) and Georg Philipp Telemann.

## Comic Opera

Comic opera emerged in the early 18th century primarily as a reaction to Italian serious opera (*opera seria*). It was a dramatic genre in which elements of humor, parody, and satire were prominent.

**General Characteristics.** Comic opera differed from serious opera in several respects: (1) Light, frivolous, and humorous subjects were used; (2) commonplace characters replaced exalted or heroic figures of serious operas; (3) except in Italian comic opera, spoken dialogue replaced the recitatives of serious opera; (4) popular tunes replaced the dramatic and formal arias; (5) ensemble finales of soloists and chorus became common features at the conclusions of acts; and (6) characters, aria texts, and melodies of serious operas were often parodied.

**Types of Comic Opera.** Comic opera was generally more indigenous than serious opera, and it developed somewhat differently in different European countries.

*Italian Opera Buffa.* Comic opera in Italy, called *opera buffa,* originated as intermezzi between acts of serious operas. Early in the 18th century it emerged as an independent form, principally in Naples. Opera buffa employed recitative more than spoken dialogue. Choral finales were typical. A famous opera buffa was *La Serva Padrona* by Giovanni Pergolesi (1710–36). Other composers were Alessandro Scarlatti and Baldassare Galuppi (1706–85).

*French Opéra Comique.* French comic opera, known as *opéra comique,* originated in the early 18th century as a form of popular entertainment consisting of tunes called *vaudevilles*. However, originally composed comic operas were not produced in France until the second half of the 18th century. An early opéra comique was *Le Devin du Village* (1752) by Jean Jacques Rousseau (1712–78).

**English Ballad Opera.** A form of comic opera, called *ballad opera*, flourished in England in the second quarter of the 18th century. They employed well known tunes, often borrowed from serious Italian operas which they parodied. The most famous ballad opera is *The Beggar's Opera* by librettist John Gay (1685–1732), with songs arranged by John Pepusch (1667–1752).

**German Singspiel.** The word *Singspiel* meant serious opera at the beginning of the 18th century. About the middle of the century it came to designate German comic opera. The first singspiels were translations of English ballad operas, but in the second half of the 18th century they were originally composed works. The principal composer was Johann Adam Hiller (1728–1804).

**Spanish Zarzuela.** Serious opera did not develop in Spain. A popular dramatic form, akin to opera buffa, was the *zarzuela*, an example of which is *Celos aun del ayre matan* by Juan Hidalgo (d. 1685).

## Vocal Chamber Music

Though less important than opera, a considerable literature of nontheatrical vocal music was composed in the Baroque. Classified as vocal chamber music, it was composed for a few performers and an intimate audience in a small room. Two general types of vocal chamber music are solo songs and chamber cantatas.

**Solo Song.** By 1600 an impressive literature of solo songs with lute accompaniment already existed in Spain and England. Solo songs continued to be composed during the Baroque, principally in Italy, Germany, and England.

**Italian Song.** The Baroque was ushered in by Italian monodies, the first collection of which was Caccini's *Le Nuove Musiche* which contained solo songs with figured bass accompaniment. Also in the early Baroque were the Italian *solo madrigals* such as Monteverdi's *Fifth Book of Madrigals*. Such works were the forerunners of the Italian secular cantata in the second half of the century.

*German Lied.* In the second half of the 17th century an important school of lied composers developed. Solo songs were often published in sets. The composers were Adam Krieger (1634–66), Johann Theile, Philipp Erlebach (1657–1714), Johann Scholze (1705–50), and Telemann.

*English Song.* Two collections of English solo songs were *Amphion Anglicus* by John Blow and *Orpheus Britannicus* by Purcell.

A favorite form among 17th-century English composers was the *catch,* an *a cappella* vocal canon or round, often based on ribald and humorously witty texts. John Blow, William Lawes (1602–45), Henry Purcell, and many lesser composers wrote catches.

**Chamber Cantata.** In the second half of the 17th century an important form of secular vocal music emerged in Italy, the *chamber cantata* (*cantata da camera*). Chamber cantatas were short, nontheatrical compositions (that is, not performed on a stage or with acting, scenery, costumes, or dialogue), based on texts of a somewhat narrative character. Composed for one or two solo voices with basso continuo accompaniment, they consisted of secco recitatives alternating with da capo arias, usually two or three of each.

*Composers.* Alessandro Scarlatti, with more than six hundred chamber cantatas, represents the summit of Italian cantata composition. Most Italian opera composers wrote cantatas, including Luigi Rossi, Giacomo Carissimi, Marc' Antonio Cesti, Giovanni Legrenzi, Alessandro Stradella, and Handel.

French chamber cantatas, which were influenced by Italian models, were composed by Marc-Antoine Charpentier (1634–1704), André Campra (1660–1744), Louis Clérambault (1676–1749), and Rameau.

German composers of chamber cantatas (*Kammerkantate*) were Reinhard Keiser, Georg Telemann, and J. S. Bach, who composed some twenty secular cantatas, the most famous of which are the *Coffee Cantata* and the *Peasant Cantata.*

In England, Henry Purcell composed nine secular cantatas for two or more voices, and, for special occasions, a large number of works called *odes,* for solo voices, chorus, and orchestra. These works fall outside the category of chamber music because of the larger resources involved.

## SCORES AND RECORDINGS

The following items listed under Serious Opera and Comic Opera are representative components (arias, duets, recitatives, choruses) rather than complete operas.

*Serious Opera*

Italian: MM 31, 44, TEM 44, HAM 182, 187, 189, 206, 208, 209, 221, 241, 244, 259, 262

French: MM 36, 41, TEM 45, HAM 223, 224, 225, 276, 277

German: TEM 46, HAM 267

English: HAM 204 (masque) 243, 255, 290

*Comic Opera:* TEM 50, HAM 222, 264, 285, 286, 287, 291

*Solo Song* (not including arias from operas): MM 30, HAM 184, 205, 228, 254

*Chamber Cantata:* TEM 49, HAM 213, 258, 273

# CHAPTER 15

# *Religious Music*

Although overshadowed and strongly influenced by opera, religious music constituted a significant portion of baroque literature. It falls in two broad classes: *liturgical* and *nonliturgical* music.

## Liturgical Music

Liturgical music, composed for a functional part of a church service, continued to develop in both branches of Christian religion. The forms and styles of opera permeated Catholic and Protestant music alike.

**Catholic Music.** More than any other type of music, Catholic music manifested baroque dualism. Throughout the 17th century the conservative *stile antico* existed side by side with *stile moderno,* often in the works of a single composer.

**Mass and Motet.** Settings of the Ordinary and motets for the Proper and Offices were composed in both styles. The *a cappella* tradition was preserved in the Sistine Chapel in Rome, and elsewhere there were strong adherents of the renaissance polyphonic style. On the other hand, Masses and motets were also composed in the new dramatic style, often musically indistinguishable from opera. They used solo voices (e.g., arias, duets), concertato effects with one or more choruses, and instrumental groups; but there was no place for recitative in the Mass. Polychoral writing, which began in the Venetian school late in the 16th century, was not neglected in the 17th century.

*Schools and Composers.* The earliest example of nuove musiche church music, *Cento Concerti Ecclesiastici* composed in 1602 by Lodovico Grossi da Viadana (1564–1645), was a collection of a "hundred church pieces" for one or more solo voices with basso continuo. An example of imposing baroque style was a festival Mass composed by Orazio Benevoli (1605–72) in fifty-three parts, for two eight-part choruses, soloists, and instrumental choirs with basso continuo. Most Italian opera composers wrote church music. An example of late-baroque dramatic style is Alessandro Scarlatti's *Missa di Santa Cecilia.*

Munich, Salzburg, Prague, and Vienna became important centers of church music outside Italy. Among numerous Italian and Austrian composers were Monteverdi at San Marco in Venice, Christopher Strauss (c. 1580–1631), Johann Stadlmayr (c. 1560–1648), Giovanni Valentini (d. 1649), Antonio Bertali (1605–69), Johann Schmelzer (c. 1623–88), Johann Kerll (1627–93), Antonio Draghi (1635–1715), Marc Antonio Ziani (c. 1653–1715), Alessandro Scarlatti, Giovanni Pergolesi, Antonio Caldara (c. 1670–1736), and Johann Fux, who was one of the more conservative composers and the author of a famous treatise on counterpoint entitled *Gradus ad Parnassum.* Perhaps the greatest, and certainly the most famous, masterpiece in all baroque Catholic music is Bach's *Mass in B Minor.*

French composers of Catholic music, mostly motets in cantata form, were Lully, Marc-Antoine Charpentier, Michel Richard de Lalande (1657–1726), and François Couperin.

**Protestant Music.** The main developments in Protestant church music took place in Germany.

*Church Cantata.* The principal form of Protestant church music was the *church cantata* (*Kirchenkantate*), which became an integral part of the Lutheran service in the second half of the 17th century. Texts were taken from chorales and biblical passages. In the early 18th century, Erdmann Neumeister (1671–1756) and others wrote cycles of cantata texts. There were solo cantatas for one or more voices with continuo accompaniment, and there were cantatas on a larger scale employing solo voices (arias, duets), recitative, chorus, and orchestra. Chorale melodies were used extensively in choruses and in some arias. Lutheran cantatas concluded with the singing of the chorale by congregation and choir.

*Composers.* The leading composer of German Protestant music in the 17th century was Heinrich Schütz. His church music, in diverse forms and styles, ranged from conservative renaissance-style motets to polychoric music and larger works that approached the cantata form. He made little use of chorale melody. His most important works include Latin motets (*Cantiones Sacrae*), German motets for solo voices with organ accompaniment (*Kleine Geistliche Konzerte*), and *Symphoniae Sacrae* for various media.

Schütz's predecessors were Hassler, Praetorius, Schein, and Scheidt. Middle- and late-baroque composers were Franz Tunder (1614–67), Andreas Hammerschmidt (1611–75), Buxtehude, Pachelbel, Johann Kuhnau (1660–1722), and Telemann. The ultimate master of the church cantata was J. S. Bach, who composed over 200 cantatas.

*English Church Music.* Anglican Services and anthems continued to be composed in the Baroque. The older cathedral anthem in renaissance motet style and the later verse anthem reflected baroque dualism. Although they used solo voices, chorus, and instrumental accompaniment, verse anthems were more conservative and less influenced by opera than most church music on the Continent. Principal composers were John Blow, Henry Purcell, Pelham Humfrey (1647–74), and William Croft (1678–1727).

**Instrumental Church Music.** Two forms of instrumental church music, the organ chorale prelude and the church sonata, will be discussed under organ music and chamber music, respectively, in the following chapter.

## Nonliturgical Music

Nonliturgical music is that based on religious subjects but not intended to be performed as part of a church service. The principal category of nonliturgical music is *oratorio*.

**Oratorio.** About the middle of the 17th century, oratorio emerged as a religious form distinct from opera and liturgical music.

*Components.* In its mature form, oratorio employed most of the components of opera: arias and duets for solo voices, recitative, chorus, overture, and other instrumental pieces; but, except in its earliest stages, it made no use of dramatic action, staging, scenery, or costumes. Oratorio differs from opera in two additional respects: it employs a *narrator* (called *testo* or *historicus*) who tells the religious story in recitative, and it makes considerably more use of chorus.

Two types of Italian oratorios were the *oratorio Latino*, with Latin texts, and *oratorio volgare*, with Italian texts. The former disappeared in the second half of the 17th century.

*Origins.* Religious plays with music were common in the Middle Ages and Renaissance. In the late 16th century Filippo Neri, a priest, organized informal devotional meetings held in a Roman prayer chapel called the *oratory* where laudes and religious dialogues were performed. One of the latter was an allegorical play with monodic music by Emilio del Cavalieri (c. 1550–1602), entitled *The Play of Soul and Body* (*La Rappresentazione di Anima e di Corpo*), produced in Rome in 1600. This work is considered to be the earliest prototype of oratorio. Later, the religious operas of the Roman school, such as Landi's *Santo Alessio,* approached the realization of true oratorio except that they were fully staged theater works.

*Composers.* The first composer of oratorios was Giacomo Carissimi (1605–74), whose *Jephte, Judicium Salomonis,* and others were composed on Latin texts.

Marc-Antoine Charpentier, a French pupil of Carissimi, wrote oratorios both in French and Latin (*Le Reniement de St. Pierre*). Successors of Carissimi were Antonio Draghi, Alessandro Stradella, Alessandro Scarlatti, Antonio Lotti, Antonio Caldara, and Leonardo Leo (1694–1744).

The culmination of baroque oratorio is represented by Handel, who in his later years abandoned opera for oratorio, and established a long tradition of that form in England. His eminence in the field of oratorio rests primarily on his superb mastery of choral technique. Best known among his more than twenty oratorios are *Samson, Israel in Egypt, Judas Maccabaeus, Solomon,* and the famous Christmas oratorio, *The Messiah,* composed in Dublin in 1741.

*Passion Music.* Presentation of the Easter story, the Passion, according to the gospels of the Evangelists Matthew, Mark, Luke, and John, has a long history dating back to the early Christian Era. Musical settings of the Passion sometimes have been liturgical, sometimes nonliturgical in oratorio form.

*Gospel Recitation.* From about A.D. 300 to 1100 it was common practice to have the gospels recited in church during Holy Week.

*Plainsong Passion.* In the 12th century the Passion story was presented as a play in which the part of Christ was sung in a low register by a priest, the part of the Evangelist narrator was sung in a middle register by another priest, and the part of the crowd (*turba*) was sung in a high register by a third priest. This was done in a psalmodic chant style.

*Polyphonic Passion.* In the Renaissance, composers began using polyphony, at first setting only the exclamations of the turba in motet style. Polyphonic Passions were composed by most of the 16th-century masters, including Palestrina.

*Oratorio Passion.* With the advent of dramatic styles in the 17th century, it was not long before Passions were composed in oratorio fashion. Early examples are *The Resurrection Story* and *The Seven Last Words* by Schütz.

*Chorale Passion.* The importance of the chorale in the Lutheran service ultimately affected settings of the Passion, and, early in the 18th century, chorales were added as reflective elements in oratorio Passions. A famous chorale Passion is J. S. Bach's *St. Matthew Passion* in which the chorale "O Sacred Head" by Hassler is used in this way.

**Religious Songs.** Apart from chorales and arias from oratorios and cantatas, religious solo songs constituted a relatively small and unimportant part of baroque religious music. An example of this category is a collection entitled *Arie Devote* by Ottavio Durante.

**SCORES AND RECORDINGS**
The following items are mostly selections from larger works.

*Liturgical Music*
  Catholic: HAM 185, 257, 266
  Protestant: MM 33, 46, 48, TEM 38, 43, HAM 202, 214, 242, 268, 279

*Nonliturgical Music*
  Oratorio: MM 32, 45, TEM 37, 42, HAM 183, 207, 218, 226, 272, 281
  Passion: MM 49, HAM 201
  Devotional song: HAM 200, 205, 213, 254

# CHAPTER 16

# *Instrumental Music*

During the Baroque, instrumental music for the first time became as important as vocal music, in quality as well as in quantity.

**General Characteristics.** Between 1600 and 1750 notable developments took place in various aspects of instrumental concepts and practice. Some characteristics apply more or less equally to the entire period; others evolved gradually or else made their appearance late in the period.

*Instrumental Idiom.* Although awareness of the special properties and capacities of instruments was evident to a limited extent in some renaissance music, instrumental idiom became fully recognized during the Baroque.

*Improvisation.* Improvisation became a more important discipline in the Baroque than ever before, and generally more important in instrumental than in vocal music. In addition to originally improvised music on solo instruments, it played an important role in the realization of figured bass, in ornamentation, and in improvisations on a given theme. These improvisatory aspects create problems in the performance and understanding of baroque music.

*Basso Continuo.* The basso continuo, a purely instrumental concept, lent a characteristic prominence to bass parts in all categories of ensemble music. It is one of the most distinct and consistent features of the Baroque as a whole.

*Variation.* The principle of thematic variation permeated much instrumental music, even in forms which were not primarily based on structural variation.

*Sequence.* Repetition of melodic patterns on successively higher or lower pitches, called *sequence,* became a typical feature of instrumental music in the middle Baroque. Sequential progression was often used in modulations.

*Ensemble Media.* A clearer distinction between chamber and orchestral media was established in the late 17th century.

*Tuning. Equal-tempered tuning* of keyboard instruments replaced the older method, called *just intonation* in the late Baroque. Bach's *Well-Tempered Clavier,* in two volumes, each containing twenty-four preludes and fugues in all major and minor keys, was composed partly to demonstrate equality of keys in the new system of tuning.

### Baroque Instruments

Most of the instruments used in the Renaissance continued to be used throughout the Baroque, but all underwent further mechanical improvement during the period. The violin family emerged toward the end of the 17th century.

**Keyboard Instruments.** Keyboard instruments were used for basso continuo parts and solo music which constitutes a major portion of instrumental literature. Three keyboard types were clavichord, harpsichord, and organ.

*Clavichord.* The clavichord produced tone by means of a metal wedge striking the string when the key was depressed (see Figure 10). It had a weak tone but was capable of producing delicate shades of dynamics. It was used principally in Germany and limited to solo and small ensemble music in the home.

*Harpsichord.* The harpsichord was known under several names: *clavecin* (French), *clavicembalo* (Italian), *virginal* (English, 16th and early 17th centuries), and the German words *Klavier* or *clavier* which meant either harpsichord or clavichord. The harpsichord usually had two manuals (keyboards). Its tone, produced by quills which plucked the strings mechanically when a key was depressed (see Figure 10), was stronger than that of the clavichord, but it was incapable of producing dynamic shading. Being the principal basso continuo instrument, the harpsichord was one of the most distinctive sounds in baroque ensemble music. It was perhaps the most favored medium for solo compositions.

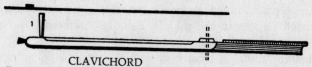

## CLAVICHORD
1. Tangent which strikes string when key is depressed.

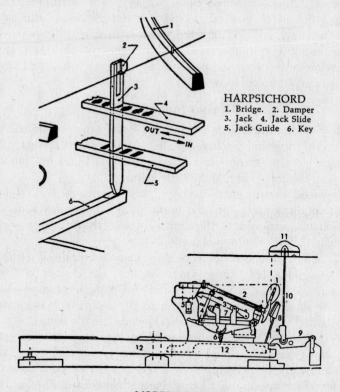

## HARPSICHORD
1. Bridge.  2. Damper
3. Jack  4. Jack Slide
5. Jack Guide  6. Key

## MODERN PIANO

1. Hammer Head.  2. Hammer Shank and Butt.  3. Repetition Lever.  4. Tack.  5. Set-off Button.  6. Capstan Screws.  7. Repetition Spring.  8. Check Head and Wire.  9. Damper Body.  10. Damper Wire.  11. Damper Head.  12. Key.

*Harpsichord reprinted by permission of the publishers from Willi Apel, Harvard Dictionary of Music, Cambridge, Mass.: Harvard University Press, 1945. Clavichord and Piano reprinted by permission of the publishers from Grove's Dictionary of Music and Musicians. New York: The Macmillan Company.*

## Figure 10
### *Action of keyboard instruments*

*Piano.* The piano, originally called *gravicembalo col piano e forte*, was invented around 1709 by Bartolommeo Cristofori (1655–1731) in Florence. Despite the significance of the new hammer and escapement action, the piano was not in general use until late in the 18th century, and virtually no baroque music was composed for this instrument.

*Organ.* The baroque organ possessed a greater variety and power of tone than the renaissance organ. It was primarily associated with church music, both as solo and accompanying instrument. There was a remarkable growth of idiomatic organ literature.

**String Instruments.** Types of string instruments in general use between 1600 and 1750 changed appreciably.

*Viols.* Instruments of the viol family were the principal strings during the 17th century, but around 1700 they were gradually being replaced by the new instruments of the violin family.

*Violin Family.* The 18th century saw viols replaced by violins, violas, and cellos. The bass viol (contrabass or double bass) was retained from the viol family. The master violin makers came from three families in Cremona, the most famous members of which were Nicolò Amati (1596–1684), Giuseppe Bartolomeo Guarneri (1698–1744), and Antonio Stradivari (1644–1737). The violin sound became the dominant timbre in late baroque ensemble music.

*Lute.* The lute lost its place of eminence during the 17th century. A small amount of lute music was composed in France and Germany. In Spain, the vihuela was replaced by the guitar.

**Wind Instruments.** The principal woodwind instruments were oboe, bassoon, and flute. The older end-blown recorders were still being used in the late Baroque, but the transverse flute was also commonly employed as a solo and ensemble instrument.

Brass instruments included various kinds of trumpets, horns, and trombones which were employed mostly in large ensembles, rarely as solo instruments.

**Percussion Instruments.** Timpani were the only percussion instruments in general use, and they were employed only in unusually large orchestras.

## Instrumental Forms

Most instrumental forms in the first half of the 17th century were those first developed in the Renaissance. New forms emerged in the second half of the century.

**Terminology.** It must be emphasized that form terminology in the Baroque was often loosely applied and ambiguous. A given term sometimes implied one type in the early Baroque and something quite different later on. In some instances a single term was applied to several different forms, in others different terms were used for one type of composition. In the following classifications it will be noted that overlapping occurs: a form name in one category may appear again in another classification.

**Fugal Forms.** In this category are contrapuntal forms based primarily on systematic imitation of one or more themes.

*Early Forms.* Forms which carried over from the Renaissance were the ricercare, canzona, fantasia and capriccio. Compositions so named were composed for keyboard instruments and ensembles. The contrapuntal fantasia was primarily for ensembles of viols. The sectional canzona was the forerunner of the sonata. After 1650 these older forms were generally replaced by the fugue.

*Fugue.* By the end of the 17th century the monothematic *fugue* (also *fuga*) had reached a certain degree of standardization. Each voice in turn introduced the theme, alternating between *subject* in the tonic key and *answer* in the dominant key. *Episodes* between statements of the subject were characteristically modulatory and sequential in structure. Within this general framework, there was much flexibility of procedure and style. Fugues were composed in all media, including choral ensembles. They were composed as independent pieces and also as movements in larger works.

**Variation Forms.** The principle of thematic variation was used in several forms outside this classification: canzona, dance suite, and cantus firmus compositions. Keyboard instruments were the principal media for variation forms. In Italy during the first half of the 17th century, variations on a popular theme were called *partitas* (a term also used later for suites). Other terms for baroque variations were *passacaglia, chaconne,* and *ground.* The latter form, used chiefly in England, was a short recurrent theme in the bass over which the counterpoint continuously changed. Pieces called passacaglia and chaconne sometimes used this plan, and other times they were somewhat free variations on a harmonic progression. Improvised variations on a ground bass were called *divisions*.

Cantus firmus variations, especially important in Germany, consisted of restatement of a chorale melody in its entirety, each statement in a different contrapuntal setting.

**Dance Suite.** As in the Renaissance, so also in the Baroque, dance music was an important category. Stylized, nonfunctional dances were mostly composed in groups called *suites* or *partitas*. Media for dance music were harpsichord, chamber ensemble, and orchestra.

*Form.* There was no standard number, type, or order of movements in the suite. With few exceptions, the movements of a suite were all in the same key. The form of individual dance movements was almost always *binary*. Baroque binary form consisted of two sections, each repeated. The first section modulated to the dominant key (or relative major); the second section began in the contrasting key and modulated back to the tonic key at the end. The dance movements most commonly appearing in the late Baroque were the *allemande* (or *allemanda*), *courante* (or *corrente*), *sarabande* (or *sarabanda*), and *gigue* (or *giga*).

*Allemande.* The allemande was usually moderately fast, in duple meter, and began with an eighth- or sixteenth-note upbeat. It was probably of German origin (*allemande* is the French word for "German").

*Courante.* The courante was in triple meter, sometimes combining or alternating $\frac{3}{2}$ and $\frac{6}{4}$ meters. It was in faster tempo than the allemande (*courant* means "running" in French). It, too, usually began with a short upbeat.

*Sarabande.* The sarabande, of Spanish origin, was in triple meter, slow tempo, and employed one or both of these rhythmic patterns: ♩. ♪ ♩ and ♩ ♩. ♪

*Gigue.* The gigue was usually the final dance in the late baroque suite. It was normally in compound triple meter ($\frac{6}{8}$, $\frac{9}{8}$, or $\frac{12}{8}$) and lively tempo. Its texture was generally more fugal than that of the other movements.

**Other Dances.** One or more of the following dances were often included in suites, usually between the sarabande and gigue: gavotte, bourrée, minuet, loure, polonaise, rigaudon, and passepied. It was not uncommon for a dance movement to be followed by an ornamental version, called a *double*.

**Nondance Movements.** Baroque suites usually began with a prelude. Other nondance movements appearing in suites were fugues, variations, and airs.

**Chorale Prelude.** The most important category of baroque organ music was the *chorale prelude*, a form of instrumental church music. The term chorale prelude is here used to include all organ compositions in which the material was derived from a chorale melody which was identified in the title. The four main types are *cantus firmus, coloration, partita,* and *fantasia.*

**Cantus Firmus.** The most common type presented the chorale melody continuously as a cantus firmus in longer note values against faster-moving counterpoint, either derived from or independent of the chorale melody. The cantus firmus could appear in any part including the pedals. In some chorale preludes the phrases of the chorale were separated by short interludes of continuing counterpoint in the accompanying parts. Another style introduced each phrase of the chorale in imitative counterpoint preceding the cantus firmus in longer notes.

**Coloration Chorale.** The type known as *coloration chorale* stated the chorale melody in the top part as a cantus firmus but in a highly ornamented version which disguised the original melody.

**Chorale Partita.** Sets of variations on a chorale tune were called *chorale partitas*. In each variation, called a *verse*, the chorale melody itself was modified or else it was kept intact as a cantus firmus while the style of accompanying counterpoint changed.

**Chorale Fantasia.** A composition in which the counterpoint in all parts was freely derived from a chorale melody was called a *chorale fantasy* (or *fantasia*). Chorale preludes of this type were sometimes written as trios with one part for each manual and a third in the pedals. These were called *chorale trios. Chorale fugues* or *fughettas* derived subjects freely from one or more phrases of a chorale which were treated in fugal style but without a continuous cantus firmus in any voice.

**Improvisatory Forms.** Keyboard compositions bearing the titles *toccata, prelude,* or *fantasia* appeared frequently in the Baroque. These terms implied no specific structure or style, nor was there any basic distinction among them. The predominant characteristic was an improvisatory effect. Such pieces variously included sections of materials such as sustained chords, rapid scales, figuration, and contrapuntal textures. They lacked any distinct thematic material and any formal unity. In the late Baroque they were often paired with a fugue in the same key, resulting in such titles as *Toccata and Fugue in D Minor* and *Fantasia and Fugue in G Minor.*

**Sonata.** No word in baroque terminology is more nondescript than *sonata.* In the course of the Baroque it had quite different implications of style, form, and medium.

*Origin.* The term *"sonada"* appeared as early as 1535 in a collection of lute music by Milan. A famous composition was Giovanni Gabrieli's *Sonata Pian' e Forte* (1597) for two choirs of brass instruments. Thus, in its early use, "sonata" meant nothing more than a composition for instrumental medium as opposed to cantata, a vocal composition.

Between 1600 and 1650 instrumental canzonas were composed in several sections contrasting in tempo and meter. These sections became longer and fewer, ultimately evolving into separate movements so that by 1650 the canzona had merged with the sonata, the latter term replacing the former.

*Media.* In the second half of the 17th century multimovement sonatas were written for small chamber media: unaccompanied solo sonatas for violin or cello, accompanied solo sonatas for different instruments with basso continuo, and *trio sonatas,* the most important chamber media in the middle and late Baroque. The latter were written on three staves for two solo instruments and basso continuo played by a cello and keyboard instrument.

*Church Sonata.* The *church sonata* (*sonata da chiesa*) evolved in Italy after 1650. It consisted of a number of movements contrasting in tempo and texture. By the late Baroque the church sonata was mostly in four movements with tempi indicated according to the plan slow-fast-slow-fast. The church sonata was intended to be performed (like ricercare, canzoni, and toccatas) in parts of the service, and it employed the organ in the continuo part. Some of the movements, especially the last, had a distinctly dancelike character, though they were not so labeled.

**Chamber Sonata.** The *chamber sonata* (*sonata da camera*), or *partita,* was in effect a suite of dance movements bearing such titles as (in Italian) allemanda, corrente, sarabanda, giga, and so on. Trio chamber sonatas employed the harpsichord for the continuo part.

In the late Baroque, the distinction between church and chamber sonata forms became less clear, and sonatas often included dance names for some movements and only tempo indications for others.

**Tower Sonatas.** In Germany in the 17th century pieces called *tower sonatas* (*Turmsonaten*) were composed for small ensembles of wind instruments. They were intended for performance at certain hours of the day from municipal towers or church steeples. This literature is represented by a collection entitled *Hora Decima* by Johann Petzel (or Petzold, 1639–94).

**Keyboard Sonatas.** Solo sonatas for harpsichord, introduced at the end of the 17th century, constitute a relatively small portion of baroque instrumental literature. Kuhnau in Germany and Domenico Scarlatti in Italy were the principal composers.

**Orchestral Music.** A clearer distinction between chamber and orchestral media became evident toward the end of the 17th century. Form terminology typically lacked standardization in such terms as sinfonia, overture, and concerto, terms which occasionally applied to smaller instrumental media.

**Orchestra.** The baroque orchestra also lacked standardization. It was composed mainly of strings; wind and percussion instruments were used sparingly. The basso continuo was consistently the bass part of the orchestra. There was generally a lack of color definition in baroque orchestration: instruments of different kinds doubled on each part.

**Concerto.** The term *concerto* was first used to designate a composition for voices with separate instrumental parts as, for example, in Viadana's *Cento Concerti Ecclesiastici.* Around the mid-17th century the term came to mean an instrumental composition in which there were opposing instrumental groups in typically baroque concertato style.

*Concerto Grosso.* The most important form of baroque orchestral music was the *concerto grosso.* It was constructed on the basis of a group of two or three solo instruments (*concertino*) opposing the full orchestra (*ripieno* or *tutti*), often in alternating and contrasting sections within a movement.

*Solo Concerto.* The latest to develop was the concerto for one instrument and orchestra. At the end of the Baroque it was standardized in a three-movement form. The fast-slow-fast plan of movements remained the structural form until the present.

*Other Orchestral Forms.* Orchestral music was also composed in the form of overtures (French ouverture and Italian sinfonia), individual dances, and dance suites. No small portion of baroque orchestral music was that written as components of operas, oratorios, and other large vocal works.

## Schools and Composers

In the following summary the most important composers are listed according to nationality and, insofar as possible, identified with particular forms of media.

**Italy.** Composers of keyboard music were Girolamo Frescobaldi (1583–1643) in the first half of the 17th century; Bernardo Pasquini (1637–1710) in the second half; and Domenico Scarlatti in the late Baroque, who composed one-movement sonatas called *essercizi.*

Principal names in instrumental ensemble music were Maurizio Cazzati (c. 1620–77), Alessandro Stradella, Giovanni Vitali (1644–92), Giuseppe Torelli (c. 1658–1709), Francesco Geminiani (1687–1762), and Arcangelo Corelli, the most important composer of middle-baroque ensemble music for strings. Antonio Vivaldi dominated the field of solo concerto music in the late Baroque. Giuseppe Tartini (1692–1770) belongs both to late baroque and preclassical violin music.

**Germany.** Two composers of lute music were Esaias Reusner (1636–97) and Leopold Weiss (1686–1750).

German composers of organ music, prominent throughout the Baroque, include Samuel Scheidt, the Dutch composer Jan Pieterszoon Sweelinck, Franz Tunder, Jan Reinken (1623–1722), Dietrich Buxtehude, Johann Philipp Krieger (1649–1725), Georg

Böhm (1661–1733), Johann Pachelbel, and Johann Kuhnau. J. S. Bach's chorale preludes in all forms, toccatas, preludes, fantasias, and fugues are the culminating works of baroque organ music.

Composers of harpsichord music were Johann Froberger, Johann Caspar Ferdinand Fischer (c. 1665–1746), whose *Ariadne Musica* of 1715 is a collection of preludes and fugues predating Bach's *Well-Tempered Clavier,* and Johann Kuhnau, whose *Frische Klavierfrüchten* of 1696 were the first harpsichord sonatas. The culmination of baroque harpsichord music is represented by Bach's suites, partitas, inventions, preludes, and fugues.

Ensemble music was composed by Johann Schein, Johann Rosenmüller (c. 1620–84), noted for solo and trio sonatas, Heinrich von Biber (1644–1704), whose fifteen solo violin sonatas employ unusual tuning of the strings called *scordatura,* Georg Muffat (1653–1704), Johann Jacob Walther (1650–c. 1717), Johann Fux, and Evaristo dall'Abaco (1675–1742). Special mention should be made of Georg Philipp Telemann, who was one of the most versatile and prolific composers of the entire Baroque, and who wrote instrumental music in all media and forms. Bach's ensemble music includes accompanied and unaccompanied solo sonatas, six *Brandenburg Concertos* (concerti grossi), four orchestral suites, and concertos for violin and one to four harpsichords. *The Musical Offering* and *The Art of the Fugue* are unique masterpieces which, along with *The Well-Tempered Clavier,* are the ultimate achievement in baroque counterpoint.

**France.** Denis Gaultier (c. 1603–72) was the principal French composer of lute music in the Baroque.

French clavecin music, noted for its rococo ornamentation (called *agréments*), delicacy, and refinement, consisted mostly of compositions in dance forms with fanciful titles. Principal names in the clavecin school were Jacques Champion de Chambonnières (c. 1602–72), Jean-Henri d'Anglebert (c. 1628–91), and François Couperin. The culmination of French harpsichord music in the late Baroque was Rameau.

Organ music was composed by Jean Titelouze, Henry Dumont (c. 1610–84), Nicolas Lebegue (1631–1702), Nicolas Gigault (c. 1625–1707), Guillaume Nivers (1632–1714), André Raison (c.

1645–1714), François Couperin, Louis Marchand (1669–1732), and Louis-Claude Daquin (1694–1772).

Marin Marais (1656–1728), viola da gambist for Louis XIV, wrote five books of pieces for that instrument. Jean-Marie Leclair (1697–1764) was the principal French composer of violin sonatas, trio sonatas, and concertos. French orchestral music from Lully to Rameau was largely dance music from operas and ballets.

**England.** The early 17th century in England was dominated by the last of the Elizabethan virginalists and the continuing tradition of ensemble music for viols. Thomas Tomkins (1572–1656) wrote keyboard pieces and string fantasias. In the latter category is also the music of John Jenkins (1592–1678), William and Henry Lawes, Matthew Locke, and Henry Purcell, whose fantasies in three, four, and five parts represent the last of the renaissance-style consort music. Purcell also composed keyboard works, sonatas for chamber ensembles, and incidental and entr'acte music for orchestra.

George Frideric Handel, though more important in the fields of opera and oratorio, composed seventeen harpsichord suites, solo sonatas for flute, recorder, violin, and oboe, and trio sonatas. His orchestral music includes twelve concerti grossi, twelve organ concertos, six oboe concertos, and the famous *Water Music* and *Fireworks Music*.

**Spain.** The only significant instrumental music in Spain in the Baroque was composed for organ by Juan Cabanilles (1644–1712), Sebastian Aguilera de Heredia (c. 1565–c. 1620), and José Elias (c. 1680–c. 1749).

**SCORES AND RECORDINGS**
> Keyboard music: MM 26, 34, 35, 37, 38, 40, 42, 47, TEM 29, 39 (lute), 40, 41, HAM 190–196, 211 (lute), 212, 215–217, 229, 231, 232, 233 (lute), 234, 236, 237, 239, 240, 247–251, 261, 265, 274, 280, 284
>
> Chamber music: MM 39, 50, TEM 36, 48, HAM 198, 199, 210, 219, 230, 238, 245, 252, 253, 256, 263, 269, 271, 275, 278
>
> Orchestral music: MM 36, 43, TEM 44, 45, 47, HAM 197, 208, 220, 223, 224, 246, 259, 260, 270, 277

# V

*The*
*Classical*
*Era*
*(1750–1820)*

The 18th century, taken as a whole, presents a confusing array of stylistic trends which overlap chronologically. It encompasses diverse concepts of musical style, form, and medium manifested in the late Baroque, the Rococo, the preclassical transition, and the mature classical period. The years from 1750 to 1820, representing the rise and culmination of classicism in music, were also marked by momentous events in general history.

**Historical Background.** The last half of the 18th century and the first quarter of the 19th century was a period marked by the rise of democratic forces manifested chiefly in the French Revolution. Other military conflicts of the era were the Seven Years' War (1756–1763), the French and Indian Wars in America, the conflict between England and the American colonies culminating in the Declaration of Independence (1776) and the American Revolution, and continuing in the War of 1812, and the Napoleonic Wars in Europe. The period known as the "Age of Reason" and the "Enlightenment" was dominated by the rationalist philosophies of Kant, Diderot, and the French Encyclopedists. Other eminent writers were Voltaire, Rousseau, Lessing, and Adam Smith, whose *The Wealth of Nations* (1776) was a milestone in economic thinking. Artists of the period were Watteau, Goya, David, Reynolds, Gainsborough, and Copley. Scientific achievements included the development of the first vaccine, and the discoveries of oxygen, hydrogen, electromagnetic induction, and ultraviolet rays. The invention of the steam engine, spinning jenny, cotton gin, electric motors and generators were factors in the Industrial Revolution, which began in England around 1760.

**Rococo.** The term *rococo* refers to a style rather than a period. It developed in France in the first half of the 18th century and was a light, elaborate, and ornate style as opposed to the ponderous and grandiose baroque style. Called *style galant* in music, it was first revealed in the works of the French clavecin school (Couperin) and other late-baroque composers (Rameau, Telemann, Domenico Scarlatti). In Germany after 1750, the gallant style became *Empfindsamer Stil,* with an added element of expressive feeling or sentimentality. The rococo was a dominant style from about 1720 to about 1775. Thus, it ran concurrently with the late Baroque, the preclassical, and early classical stages of music.

**Preclassical Music.** Music which represents the transition from the Baroque to the Classical is generally referred to as *preclassical music.* Changes in concepts of form, style, and medium took place roughly from about 1740 to 1770. No clear line of distinction can be drawn between late baroque and preclassical and early classical music. Mixtures of styles often occurred in the works of the same composers.

*Basic Changes.* The old forms of the Baroque were gradually replaced by new sectional structures. Baroque counterpoint was gradually abandoned in favor of homophonic textures. The basso continuo disappeared. New instrumental media emerged. These changes were the result of experimentation by numerous composers in different geographical regions.

*Composers.* Three of J. S. Bach's sons were eminent preclassical composers: Wilhelm Friedemann Bach (1710–84), Karl Philipp Emanuel Bach (1714–88), and Johann Christian Bach (1735–82). Giuseppe Tartini was a prolific composer of violin concertos and sonatas. Johann Quantz (1697–1773) wrote an important treatise on flute playing and composed flute sonatas and concertos.

There were four centers especially important in the rise of the classical symphony. Ignaz Holzbauer (1711–83), Johann Stamitz (1717–57), and Christian Cannabich (1731–98) belonged to the Mannheim school. The chief composer in Milan was Giovanni Battista Sammartini (or San Martini, 1701–75). In Vienna the important names were Georg Matthias Monn (1717–50), Georg Wagenseil (1715–77), and Karl Ditters von Dittersdorf (1739–

99). Johann Schobert (c. 1720–67) composed symphonies and sonatas in Paris.

Other preclassical composers were Gottlieb Muffat (1690–1770), Johann Gottlieb Graun (1703–71), Carl Heinrich Graun (1704–59), Domenico Alberti (c. 1710–40), and Leopold Mozart (1719–87), the father of Wolfgang Amadeus Mozart.

**Classicism in Music.** The adjective "classical" has a number of quite different connotations: (1) the art and literature of ancient Greece, (2) the antonym of "romantic," hence, music before the 19th century, (3) the antonym of "popular" music, and (4) in a more limited sense, the period from about the middle of the 18th century to about 1820, sometimes referred to as the "Viennese classical period." It is in the latter sense that "classical" is used in music history.

Classicism implies the ideals of the Apollonian cult of ancient Greece: objectivity, ethos, emotional restraint, and balance and clarity of form. Although these ideals are to some extent reflected in certain other periods of music history, they are most clearly evident in the classical period, and more so in instrumental than in vocal music.

**Characteristics of classical music.** In addition to these general traits, classical music developed certain specific characteristics.

*Form.* Principles of sectional structure, particularly in sonata form, were firmly established in the late 18th century. Phrase structure was characteristically clear with well-defined cadences, and phrases were shorter (most commonly four measures) than in the Baroque.

*Texture.* Classical textures were typically homophonic, with a single melodic line accompanied by nonmelodic or less melodic materials. A much favored accompaniment pattern was the so-called *Alberti bass* (named for Domenico Alberti), a broken-chord figure illustrated in Example 23.

*Example 23. Alberti bass*

Counterpoint did not entirely disappear, however; fugues and other contrapuntal forms were occasionally composed. Another aspect of classical texture was the predominance of thin, light sonorities as opposed to the predominantly massive sounds of baroque music.

*Melodic Style.* Replacing the long continuous lines of baroque music, classical melody was more compact and it had more thematic identity. Generally it was more diatonic.

*Harmony.* On the whole, classical harmony was less complex than baroque harmony. It made more use of principal triads (tonic, dominant, subdominant chords), and diatonic harmony was more typical than chromatic. Chord structure was predominantly triadic; seventh chords were used sparingly, and ninth chords not at all.

*Improvisation.* With the disappearance of the basso continuo, the art of improvisation died out. All harmony was written out. Composers more specifically and more consistently indicated ornamentation, phrasing, dynamics, and other details formerly left to the performer.

*Absolute Music.* The classical period strongly favored absolute music; that is, instrumental music which (as opposed to program music) makes no pretense of describing extra-musical things or carries descriptive or imaginative titles. Classical instrumental music bore only such inscriptions as "sonata," "symphony," and "quartet."

**Four Major Composers.** The classical period was dominated by four composers of the highest quality: Haydn, Mozart, Gluck, and Beethoven.

*Haydn.* Franz Joseph Haydn (1732–1809) was the most prolific among the four. More than any other single composer, he established the form and instrumentation of the classical symphony. His principal fields were symphony, chamber music (especially string quartets and divertimenti), concerto, piano sonata, oratorio, and church music.

*Mozart.* Wolfgang Amadeus Mozart (1756–91) is, without qualification, one of the greatest geniuses of all time. His principal fields were opera, symphony, concerto, chamber music, sonatas, and Masses.

*Gluck.* Christoph Willibald von Gluck (1714–87), the least

versatile among the four, was a master of opera and opera reform.

**Beethoven.** Ludwig van Beethoven (1770–1827), like Mozart, ranks among the supreme immortals of music. His position in music history is especially significant in that he represents the transition from late classical to romantic music, and from the domination of aristocratic patronage to individual artistic freedom. He expanded the concept of sonata form and made it a vehicle of powerful expression. He was unsurpassed in the techniques of thematic development and variation. His main areas of composition were symphony, concerto, string quartet, and piano sonata. He wrote one oratorio (*Christ on the Mount of Olives*), one opera (*Fidelio*), and one festival Mass (*Missa Solemnis*).

The most significant changes in form and medium during the classical era took place in instrumental music.

## Classical Sonata Form

The term *sonata form* will be used here to mean the basic structural plan of instrumental compositions in three or four movements. Sonata form is a concept which, with certain modifications, applies to virtually all instrumental media in the classical period: solo sonatas, chamber music, symphonies, and concertos.

**First Movement.** The classical first movement is in a fast tempo, usually marked "allegro." Its sectional structure, perhaps the most significant one-movement scheme to emerge in the 18th century, is variously called *first-movement form, sonata-allegro, developed ternary,* and *sonata form.* None of these designations is entirely satisfactory, for the plan is confined neither to first movements nor to fast tempi; it is not strictly ternary (*A B A,* with contrasting thematic material in the middle section); and "sonata form" is ambiguous because it is used to designate the plan of a multi-movement work as well as this one-movement form. To avoid this ambiguity, *sonata-allegro* will be used here to designate the structure which consists of three main sections: *exposition, development,* and *recapitulation.*

**Exposition.** The exposition in sonata-allegro form presents the thematic materials of the movement. The main theme section is presented in the key of the movement (tonic key). This material is followed by a transition called *bridge* (or *bridge passage*) which modulates to the dominant key (or relative major key if the movement is in a minor key). The *second theme* (or *subordinate theme*) is then presented in the contrasting key. The exposition may conclude with still another theme, called *closing theme*, or *codetta*. The end of the exposition is marked by a double-bar repeat sign, but in modern performances of classical symphonies the exposition is usually not repeated.

**Development.** There is no standard practice in regard to procedures followed in the development section. It utilizes any or all of the material from the exposition which is "developed" in various ways. Themes or motives therefrom are presented in different keys, registers, textures, and (in symphonies) timbres. The development section may also contain any number of nonthematic episodes. It concludes in the tonic key and moves without pause into the recapitulation.

**Recapitulation.** The recapitulation is a restatement of the exposition but with all subsections remaining in the tonic key.

**Optional Sections.** The first movement sometimes begins with an *introduction* in slow tempo. Introductions do not normally introduce the thematic material of the movement. Sonata-allegro movements quite often conclude with a *coda* which follows the closing theme of the recapitulation.

**Second Movement.** The classical second movement has three characteristics: (1) it is in slow tempo (e.g., adagio, lento); (2) it is in a contrasting key, usually the subdominant or dominant key in relation to the key of the work as a whole; and (3) it has a more lyric style than the other movements. Forms commonly used in second movements are ternary (A B A), rounded binary (A A B A), theme and variations, sonatine (sonata-allegro without a development section), and sonata-allegro.

**Third Movement.** The normal third movement in a classical four-movement work is called *menuetto* (minuet). It is in the tonic key, three-four meter, and a moderately fast tempo. It is a ternary structure, called *song form and trio,* in three main sections: minuet, trio, and minuet repeated. Each section is a rounded binary form. Thus, the minuet movement normally follows this plan:

Minuet          Trio          Minuet ("da capo")

$a$:‖:$ba$:‖     $c$:‖:$dc$:‖     $a\ b\ a$ (played without repeats)

The trio is often in a contrasting or relative key to the minuet and has a lighter texture.

In a few Haydn works and in most Beethoven compositions in sonata form, the third movement is called *scherzo*. It follows the same sectional structure, tempo, and meter as the minuet but is in a more whimsical, playful, or humorous style.

The order of the two middle movements was sometimes reversed so that the minuet or scherzo came second and the slow movement third. The minuet or scherzo was omitted in three-movement compositions.

**Fourth Movement.** The last movement, the *finale,* in a classical three- or four-movement work is in the tonic key, lively tempo, and usually in sonata-allegro form or else a rondo structure ($A\ B\ A\ C\ A$ or $A\ B\ A\ C\ A\ B\ A$).

## *The Symphony*

The classical symphony was one of the major achievements of the 18th century in terms of form and medium.

**Form.** The prototype of the classical symphony was the Italian overture form called sinfonia. In the early 18th century the sinfonia was a three-section form, fast-slow-fast. As an orchestral composition independent of opera it emerged as three separate movements in the same order of tempi. Among preclassical composers it gradually took on the internal movement structures of sonata form. A minuet was added as third movement in a four-movement work.

**Orchestra.** Two approaches to symphonic media are: (1) *instrumentation* (the instruments specified in an orchestral score) and (2) *orchestration* (the manner in which those instruments are employed).

**Instrumentation.** By the end of the 18th century the symphony orchestra consisted of four woodwind instruments in pairs (flutes, oboes, clarinets, and bassoons); trumpets, horns, and timpani, also in pairs; and a string choir consisting of first and second violins, violas, cellos, and string basses.

*Orchestration.* Strings were still the dominant color. First violins carried the burden of thematic material. Second violins and violas were most often assigned harmonic material. Cellos and basses were almost consistently doubled, written as one part on the same staff, but the basses sounding an octave lower than the cellos. Brass instruments, without valves, were almost entirely confined to tutti passages and to harmonic rather than melodic or thematic material.

**Composers.** The enormous output of symphonic literature by preclassical composers provided the foundation on which the classical symphonies of Haydn, Mozart, and Beethoven were created.

*Haydn.* Haydn wrote more than a hundred symphonies, the earliest of which belong to preclassical form and orchestration. He favored slow introductions to his first movements.

*Mozart.* Mozart's output was forty-one symphonies, among which the most famous are the last four: the *Prague Symphony* (No. 38 in D), No. 39 in E Flat, No. 40 in G Minor, and No. 41 in C (nicknamed the *Jupiter Symphony*).

*Beethoven.* Beethoven's nine symphonies transcend classical form and style; only the first and possibly the eighth are predominantly classical. As he did in other media, Beethoven expanded sonata form and infused it with his dynamic personality. In four of his symphonies (the third, fifth, sixth, and ninth) he added instruments to classical instrumentation. His Symphony No. 6, called the *Pastorale Symphony*, in five movements, was the first programmatic symphony. The Ninth Symphony, which departed still further from classical tradition, was scored for a number of additional instruments (piccolo, contrabassoon, four horns, three trombones, triangle, cymbals, and bass drum), and for solo voices and chorus in the finale.

## The Concerto

The solo concerto carried over from the Baroque but it differed in style and structure of movements.

**Form.** The classical concerto, like the baroque solo concerto, was in three movements, following the same fast-slow-fast plan. Unlike the classical symphony, it omitted the minuet movement.

*First Movement.* The first movement of the classical concerto was in sonata-allegro form but with some notable differences. There were two separate expositions: the first introduced the principal themes by the orchestra alone, and all in the tonic key; in the second exposition the solo instrument carried the thematic material in a more brilliant and ornamental version. Generally, the development and recapitulation followed the sonata-allegro procedure. Near the end of the recapitulation a *cadenza* was played by the solo instrument alone. Cadenzas were freely improvised as a virtuoso development of themes. In the 19th century, cadenzas came to be written out beforehand by the composer or by the performer.

**Second Movement.** The second movement of the concerto, like that of the symphony, was in a contrasting key and slow tempo. Its style was more lyric and less virtuosic than either the first or last movements.

**Third Movement.** The concerto finale was most commonly in rondo form, and a lively tempo. Its style was somewhat lighter than the other movements. Occasionally a cadenza was included.

**Composers.** The principal concerto literature of the classical period was composed by Haydn: twenty for piano, nine for violin, six for cello, and concertos for flute, baryton, horn, clarino, and trumpet; by Mozart: twenty-five for piano, eight for violin, and other concertos for violin and viola, bassoon, flute, flute and harp, horn, and clarinet; and by Beethoven: five for piano, among which the last, nicknamed the *Emperor,* is the most famous; and one Violin Concerto in D Major.

## Chamber Music

As distinct from orchestral medium, chamber music is composed for small ensembles consisting of only a few players and usually only one instrument to a part. It was an especially significant category of music literature in the classical period.

**Divertimento.** Compositions variously called *divertimento, serenade,* and *cassation* were written in great quantities during the preclassical and classical eras. There was apparently no distinction of meaning among the three terms. They were composed for various media ranging from small chamber ensembles to small orchestras. The number of movements ranged from three to ten and included minuets, other dances, marches, and standard sonata-form movements. Intended mostly for informal entertainment and outdoor performance, they were in a lighter and less sophisticated style than symphonies. Haydn wrote over sixty and Mozart about thirty compositions in this category.

**String Quartet.** By far the most favored chamber medium in the classical period was the string quartet consisting of two violins, viola, and cello. String quartets were written in four-movement classical sonata form. The principal composers of classical string quartets were Luigi Boccherini (1743–1805), Haydn, Mozart, and Beethoven.

**Other Chamber Media.** Instrumental combinations less extensively employed in the classical period were the mixed quartet (three string instruments and one other instrument, usually piano, flute, clarinet, or oboe), string trio and mixed trio, string quintet, and mixed quintet.

The sonata for violin and piano was less important in the classical period. The piano more often played the dominant role, the violin functioning almost as an obbligato instrument. Haydn wrote twelve violin sonatas, Mozart thirty-five, and Beethoven ten.

**Keyboard Music.** Solo sonatas for harpsichord or piano constituted an important literature in the preclassical period, especially the sonatas by Karl Philipp Emanuel Bach, Wilhelm Friedemann Bach, Johann Christian Bach, and Domenico Paradisi (or Paradies, 1710–1792). The fifty-two piano sonatas by Haydn and the seventeen by Mozart are mostly three-movement works without a minuet. Beethoven's thirty-two piano sonatas represent the culmination of that form . In addition to sonatas, Mozart wrote fifteen sets of variations, and Beethoven twenty-one sets.

# CHAPTER 19

# Opera and Religious Music

The distinction between baroque and classical styles is less clearly marked in large vocal forms than in instrumental music. While classical instrumental music holds a prominent place in today's repertory, relatively few operas, oratorios, and church compositions, among the prodigious quantity composed, are heard today.

## Opera

Neapolitan opera, which dominated the first half of the 18th century, began to merge with preclassical developments around 1720 which was also the beginning of opera reform.

**Opera Seria.** Italian *opera seria* (serious opera) had deteriorated into an artificial kind of production in which musical formality and showiness took precedence over dramatic considerations. Reactions to this situation were evident well before the mid-18th century. The first treatise to recognize abuses in Italian opera was a satire by Benedetto Marcello, published in 1720, entitled *Il Teatro Alla Moda* (*The Fashionable Theater*). Reforms, however, did not occur suddenly, nor were they universally adopted by 18th-century composers.

*Aspects of Reform.* Characteristics which represent departures from early 18th-century practice are found in some, but by no means all, operas in the second half of the century. (1) There was greater concern for the dramatic aspects of opera, less attention to formal musical aspects. (2) Structures became more flexible with the trend away from stereotyped operas consisting mainly of chains of arias. (3) Rigid da capo arias appeared less frequently, and gave way to more diversified forms. (4) Secco recitatives were less favored than more melodic recitatives with orchestral accompaniment (*recitativo strumento* or *recitativo accompagnato*). (5) Choral ensembles were more frequently employed. (6) The orchestra, no longer relegated to mere accompanying function, assumed a more expressive role. (7) Ostentatious virtuosity was less evident, and solo singers began to lose some of their autocratic domination over opera performance.

**Composers.** The first composers to reflect limited reforms were Niccolò Jommelli (1714–74) and Tommaso Traetta (1727–79). The central figure in opera reform was Gluck. After composing some twenty Italian operas in the prevailing style, he put reform ideas into practice with *Orfeo ed Euridice* in 1762. In the preface to his next opera, *Alceste,* he summarized his objectives of reform. His operas also represented the classical ideal of simplicity. Avoiding the absurd and complex plots of the time, Gluck set to music the simplified classical librettos of Calzabigi. The quality of Gluck's music raised opera to a new artistic level while at the same time it wholly served the drama. His later operas, all produced in Paris, were *Iphigénie en Aulide, Armide,* and *Iphigénie en Tauride.*

Other composers, roughly contemporary with Gluck but not in the current of reform, were Johann Adolph Hasse (1699–1783), who was probably the most popular and successful composer of his time, Niccolò Piccini (1728–1800), Giuseppe Sarti (1729–1802), Antonio Sacchini (1730–86), Johann Christian Bach, Etienne-Nicolas Méhul (1763–1817); Luigi Cherubini (1760–1842), whose principal operas were *Médée* and *Les Deux Journées;* and Gasparo Spontini (1774–1851), who wrote *La Vestal.*

Two important librettists were Pietro Metastasio (1698–1782) and Raniero Calzabigi (1714–95).

**Comic Opera.** The forms of comic opera were established during the first half of the 18th century: *opera buffa* in Italy, *opéra comique* in France, *ballad opera* in England, *Singspiel* in Germany, and *zarzuela* in Spain. These forms continued to flourish in the second half of the 18th century and were given added impetus as a kind of popular revolt against Italian opera seria.

*Italy.* In the preclassical and classical periods opera buffa developed a rapid style of nearly spoken recitative called *parlando.* Ensemble finales were characteristic. Toward the end of the 18th century, elements of opera seria appeared in buffa operas. Principal composers were Piccini (*La Buona Figliuola*), Giovanni Paisiello (1740–1816), who wrote *Nina,* Domenico Cimarosa (1749–1801), whose *Il Matrimonio Segreto* was his most popular work, and Mozart.

*France. Opéra comique* used spoken dialogue instead of recitative. It began to acquire romantic and sentimental qualities. Social and political subjects were frequently introduced. Principal composers were Egidio Duni (1709–75), François André Danican-Philidor (1726–95), Pierre-Alexandre Monsigny (1729–1817), and André Ernest Modeste Grétry (1741–1813), whose *Richard Coeur-de-Lion* was a forerunner of romantic 19th-century "rescue" operas.

*England.* After a heyday of ballad opera in the first half of the 18th century, there was a decline of opera in England. Thomas Augustine Arne (1710–78) wrote some rather sentimental operas.

*Germany.* The one important composer of German singspiel operas was Johann Adam Hiller.

*Spain.* In Spain the *tonadilla,* comparable to Italian opera buffa, superseded the older zarzuela of the early 18th century. Principal composers were Luis Mison (d. 1766), Pablo Estave (born c. 1730), and Blas Laserna (1751–1816).

**Mozart.** The pinnacle of 18th-century opera was attained by Mozart. His immortality in this field rests not on reform but on the consummate greatness of his music and his phenomenal sense of theater. Among the thousands of operas produced in the 18th century, Mozart operas are the only standard repertory today. *Idomeneo* and *The Mercy of Titus* (*La Clemenza di Tito*) are opera seria. His German operas are *The Abduction from the Seraglio* (*Die Entführung aus dem Serail*) and *The Magic Flute* (*Die Zauberflöte*). His most famous buffa operas are *The Marriage of Figaro* (*Le Nozze di Figaro*) and *So Do They All* (*Così Fan Tutte*). *Don Giovanni,* called a *dramma giocoso,* is a mixture of opera seria and opera buffa elements.

## Religious Music

From 1750 to 1820, religious music was much less important than instrumental music and opera. As in the late Baroque, it was almost completely dominated by opera styles and forms.

**Oratorio.** With a few exceptions, oratorio was an empty tradition after Handel. Relatively few works of lasting value were composed. After about 1780, oratorios were almost indistinguishable from operas; some were even staged and acted in costume. The most important works of the period were Karl Heinrich Graun's *Der Tod Jesu,* Karl Philipp Emanuel Bach's *The Israelites in the Wilderness,* and Haydn's *The Return of Tobias* and *The Creation,* which was based on Genesis and an adaptation of Milton's *Paradise Lost. The Seasons* is a secular oratorio. Haydn's oratorios, like those of most other composers in the second half of the 18th century, show a strong influence of Handel.

**Church Music.** The influence of opera on church music was even more strongly manifested than it was in the late Baroque. Nearly all composers of classical church music were opera composers. Masses were opera-like compositions for solo voices, chorus, and orchestra. Arias and duets were in no way different from those in opera except for the texts. Generally, there was a strong secular element in the style. Some baroque factors persisted in church music: fugal choruses and basso continuo parts. Even symphonic forms were occasionally employed in Masses.

Principal composers were Johann Adolph Hasse, Paisiello, with some 103 church compositions, Nicola Zingarelli (1752–1837) with over 500 works, Sarti, and Cherubini. The three great classical masters contributed to the literature of Catholic Masses. Haydn wrote some fourteen Masses, among which the *Lord Nelson Mass* is the best known. Mozart wrote some fifteen Masses, which include the Mass in C Minor, the *Coronation Mass,* and his last masterpiece, the *Requiem Mass.* Beethoven's only significant work in this category was the *Missa Solemnis.*

# VI

*The
Romantic
Era*

# CHAPTER 20

# General Considerations

The 19th century is generally known as the Romantic era, but aspects of romanticism appeared before 1800 and continued well into the 20th century.

**Historical Background.** The cultural, economic, political, and social orders of the 19th century were affected by strides in science and engineering: photography, food canning, the railway and steamboat, steel production, electricity, the telephone, telegraph, and other innovations. The spread of technology augmented the Industrial Revolution in Europe which, in turn, created new social and economic problems: the growth of capitalism and the advent of socialism, a pioneer of which was Karl Marx. Nineteenth-century conflicts were the Crimean War (1854–56), the Civil War in the United States (1861–65), and the Franco-Prussian War (1870–71). The most important movement in art was French Impressionism, beginning in the second half of the century and represented by Manet, Degas, Monet, Renoir, Pissaro, and the sculptor Rodin. Allied with this movement were the French symbolist poets Verlaine, Mallarmé, and Rimbaud. The principal philosophers were the Germans Hegel, Schopenhauer, and Nietzsche. It was a period of great romantic literature: in Great Britain, Byron, Wordsworth, Scott, Thackeray, Dickens, Hardy, Carlyle, Coleridge, and Keats were prominent; in Germany, Schiller, Goethe, Richter, Heine, Novalis, Tieck, and E. T. A. Hoffmann (romantic novelist, painter, and composer); in France, Lamartine, Musset, Hugo, and Flaubert; in America, Emerson, Longfellow, Poe, Hawthorne, and Mark Twain.

**Romanticism.** Being a composite of numerous diverse qualities, romanticism defies concise definition. In the romantic-classic dichotomy, it is expressed as the first term, and classicism as the second term, in each of the following pairs of opposites: pathos-ethos, subjectivity-objectivity, emotionalism-rationalism, and an extension of the Dionysian-Apollonian ideals of ancient Greece. Further, the 19th century was a period which was characterized both by individualism and nationalism. It was an age which yearned for the unattainable and which had a penchant for the strange, mysterious, supernatural, and the remote both in time and place. These characteristics were manifested in 19th-century philosophy, literature, art, and music.

**General Characteristics of Music.** A number of features of 19th-century music in varying degrees set it apart from other periods: (1) All the aforementioned general attributes of romanticism were evident in 19th-century music. (2) Composers became socially and economically more independent; they no longer depended on the patronage of church and aristocracy. (3) Music was generally composed for two kinds of audiences—those of the concert hall and opera house on the one hand, and the intimate salon on the other. (4) There were notable extremes of length in composition: extensive works (symphonies, concertos, operas) and miniatures (solo songs, piano pieces). (5) Composers developed a greater individuality of style than ever before. (6) They felt an affinity with poetry, literature, and art; hence, program music was a favorite type. (7) Virtuosity was a familiar trait in instrumental music; the virtuoso composer-performer was a much admired musician. (8) Preferred media were the solo song with piano accompaniment, opera, piano, and symphony orchestra; chamber and choral media were less favored. (9) Nationalism was a significant trend: composers consciously fostered national styles by using folklore as subjects for operas, songs, and program music, and by incorporating folk tunes and folk styles in their compositions. Sometimes they borrowed national styles from other countries.

**Specific Musical Characteristics.** In addition to the above characteristics, there were significant developments in compositional styles and techniques.

*Melody.* Romantic melody generally has qualities of personal warmth and expressiveness, a more lyric style, and more flexible phrase structure.

*Harmony.* Harmony was found to be an important vehicle for romantic expression. The 19th century saw expansion of harmonic idiom in terms of chord structure and progression. Dissonance was more extensive and more freely treated; seventh and ninth chords appeared more frequently. Chromaticism and modulation played important roles.

*Tonality.* 19th-century music was still basically tonal (in a central key), but key feeling, often obscured by extended chromatic modulations and the use of remotely related keys, became less distinct toward the end of the century, a trend which paved the way for radically new concepts of tonality in the 20th century.

*Texture.* Romantic textures, as in classical music, were still basically homophonic. Counterpoint, when used, was of secondary importance. In terms of sonority, 19th-century music was notable for a marked increase in richness of sound.

*Dynamics.* Romantic composers discovered the inherent possibilities of dynamics for emotional expression. Wider range of dynamic levels between loud and soft and more extensive use of crescendo and diminuendo were characteristic of the period.

*Form.* Musical form was less important than content and subjective expression. Consequently, sectional structures were generally freer, more variable, and often less distinct than in the classical era. Although sonata-allegro and other classical forms were still employed, they were much more flexible.

**The Rise of Musicology.** The romantic desire to know more about the past stimulated the rise of a scholarly discipline known as *musicology,* which involves research in music history and transcription of manuscripts into modern notation. Pioneers in musicology were Raphael Georg Kiesewetter (1773–1850), Karl Friedrich Chrysander (1826–1901), Hermann Kretzschmar (1848–1924), Hugo Riemann (1849–1919), Guido Adler (1855–1941), Peter Wagner (1865–1931), Johannes Wolf (1869–1947), and Friedrich Lüdwig (1872–1930).

## Summary of Major Composers

The following summary lists the foremost masters of 19th-century music according to nationality and points out the major fields of each composer.

**Germany and Austria.** Germany and Austria were the leading countries in 19th-century romantic music.

*Ludwig van Beethoven* (*1770–1827*): transition from classical to romantic styles; symphony, concerto, piano sonatas and variations, chamber music.

*Carl Maria von Weber* (*1786–1826*): German romantic opera.

*Franz Peter Schubert* (*1797–1828*): Viennese composer of songs, symphonies, piano sonatas, chamber music.

*Felix Mendelssohn-Bartholdy* (*1809–47*), more commonly known as *Mendelssohn:* composer, conductor; especially important in choral music and oratorio; also lied, symphony, piano music.

*Robert Schumann* (*1810–56*): composer, pianist, critic, author, and editor of the *Neue Zeitschrift für Musik* (*New Musical Journal*); lied, piano music, symphony, and concerto.

*Franz Liszt* (*1811–86*): Hungarian born, the most famous virtuoso pianist-composer of the century; innovator of symphonic poem; piano music, programmatic symphonic works; also lied, concerto, choral and organ music.

*Richard Wagner* (*1813–83*): music drama (opera), author of treatises on opera theory.

*Anton Bruckner* (*1824–96*): Austrian composer; symphony, religious choral music.

*Johannes Brahms* (*1833–97*): leading classicist among romantic composers; nonprogrammatic instrumental works; religious and secular choral music, lied, symphony, chamber and piano music.

*Gustav Mahler* (*1860–1911*): late-romantic Austrian composer of gigantic symphonic works, songs, and song cycles.

*Richard Strauss* (*1864–1949*): post-romantic composer of symphonic poems, operas, lieder.

**Italy.** Italian music was almost entirely confined to opera; instrumental music and solo song outside of opera were virtually nonexistent.

*Gioacchino Rossini* (*1792–1868*): principally opera buffa.

*Gaetano Donizetti* (*1797–1848*): romantic serious operas.

*Vincenzo Bellini* (*1801–35*): operas; noted for elegance and lyric charm.

*Giuseppe Verdi (1813–1901)*: the culminating figure of 19th-century Italian opera; *Requiem Mass.*

**France.** Musical activity in France was principally in *opéra comique* and lyric opera. In the second half of the century there was a notable rise of interest in solo song and symphonic composition.

*Giacomo Meyerbeer (1791–1864)*: grand opera.

*Hector Berlioz (1803–69)*: theory and practice of orchestration; program symphony, opera.

*Frédéric Chopin (1810–49)*: Polish-born composer of piano music.

*Camille Saint-Saëns (1835–1921)*: Symphony, opera, oratorio.

*Charles Gounod (1818–93)*: lyric opera, church music.

*César Franck (1822–90)*: Belgian-born composer and organist; organ music, symphonic works, choral music.

*Georges Bizet (1838–75)*: opera, symphonic music.

*Emmanuel Chabrier (1841–94)*: symphonic works.

*Gabriel Fauré (1845–1924)*: solo song, piano music, chamber music, *Requiem.*

*Vincent d'Indy (1851–1931)*: teacher, composer; operas, symphonic works.

*Claude Debussy (1862–1918)*: French impressionist composer; symphonic works; piano music, solo song.

**England.** From the time of Handel until the end of the 19th century, there was a dearth of first-rank composers in England comparable in stature to those on the Continent.

*Samuel Wesley (1766–1837)*: organ and church music.

*Samuel Sebastian Wesley (1810–76)*: son of Samuel Wesley; church music.

*John Field (1782–1837)*: Irish-born composer of piano music; possible influence on Chopin nocturne style.

*William Sterndale Bennett (1816–75)*: piano and orchestral works.

*John Stainer (1840–1901)*: cantatas, anthems.

*Arthur Sullivan (1842–1900)*: with poet-librettist William Gilbert, creator of famous operettas.

*Charles Hubert Parry (1848–1918)*: oratorios, anthems.

*Charles Stanford (1852–1924)*: Irish nationalist composer; church music, oratorio, opera, chamber music.

*Edward Elgar* (*1857–1934*): first of the important 20th-century English composers; orchestral works, oratorios, cantatas.

**Russia.** Russia became one of the prominent musical nations in the second half of the 19th century, with music of a strongly national flavor. "The Five," a group of composers who championed Russian nationalism, including Mussorgsky, Borodin, Balakirev, Cui, and Rimsky-Korsakov, were of great importance.

*Mikhail Glinka* (*1804–57*): nationalist opera.

*Modeste Mussorgsky* (*1839–81*): symphonic works, opera, song.

*Alexander Borodin* (*1833–87*): symphonic works, opera.

*Mily Balakirev* (*1837–1910*): symphony, song, piano music.

*César Cui* (*1835–1918*): French-born, the least important among "The Five"; songs, piano music.

*Nicolas Rimsky-Korsakov* (*1844–1908*): master of orchestration; opera, symphonic music.

*Peter Ilich Tchaikovsky* (*also, Chaikovsky, Tschaikowsky; 1840–93*): symphonic music, opera, song.

*Sergei Rachmaninoff* (*1873–1943*): the last of the great romantic pianist-composers; symphonic works, concertos, piano music.

**Norway.** Norway boasts one famous romantic composer.

*Edvard Grieg* (*1843–1907*): Norwegian nationalist; orchestra, piano, and choral works.

**Finland.**

*Jean Sibelius* (*1865–1957*): Finnish nationalist; symphonies and tone poems.

**Czechoslovakia.** Czech national music was represented by two major composers.

*Bedřich Smetana* (*1824–84*): opera, symphonic and chamber works.

*Antonin Dvořák* (*1841–1904*): symphony, chamber music.

**Spain.** The principal characteristic of romantic Spanish music is a strongly national color.

*Isaac Albéniz* (*1860–1909*): piano and symphonic music.

*Enrique Granados* (*1867–1916*): piano music, operas, symphonic works.

All aspects of romanticism permeated 19th-century opera. Especially characteristic were the rise of nationalism, the use of romantic subjects, and the emotional treatment of them. Significant changes in structure and style took place. The main centers of operatic activity were Italy, France, and Germany.

## *Italy*

Since its inception at the beginning of the 17th century, opera had held the center of musical interest and had become a tradition firmly implanted in the life of the Italian people. Opera was Italy's only important contribution to music; other fields were almost totally neglected.

**General Characteristics.** (1) Because of its strong national tradition, Italian opera was more conservative and less subject to romantic innovations than in northern countries. (2) The distinction between opera seria and opera buffa was maintained well into the century, but the latter was unimportant in the second half. (3) Gluck's reforms had virtually no effect on Italian opera, but some French influence was evident in the growing importance of the orchestra and orchestral color, and more use of chorus. (4) There was a better balance between drama and music as dramatic truth once again became an established objective. (5) Italian composers generally avoided plots based on supernatural and bizarre subjects. (6) Serious operas were mostly melodramas with violent emotional situations; escape, rescue, and redemption were typical themes. (7) Melody was the all-important vehicle for dramatic and romantic expression. (8) Shallow virtuosity was less prominent than in the 18th century. (9) Dramatic and musical continuity increased, though it was less evident in Italian opera than in Germany.

**Composers.** There were fewer first-rank composers and they were far less prolific, but more 19th- than 18th-century operas remain in the repertory.

*Rossini.* Rossini's music retained traces of classical style: clarity and simplicity of texture and form. His greatest gift was in opera buffa. Principal works were *L'Italiana in Algeri, The Barber of Seville* ( *Il Barbiere di Siviglia* ), a masterpiece of sparkling wit and comedy, and *The Thieving Magpie* ( *La Gazza Ladra* ). *William Tell,* produced in Paris, is a French grand opera.

*Bellini.* Bellini's eleven operas are serious operas, generally of high emotional content. His lyric style is said to have influenced Chopin's melody. His best known works are *The Sleepwalker* ( *La Sonnambula* ), *Norma,* and *The Puritans* ( *I Puritani* ).

*Donizetti.* The most prolific among the triumvirate who dominated Italian opera before 1850, Donizetti wrote some seventy operas, which include serious and comic operas. He is best known for *Lucia di Lammermoor,* a romantic melodrama containing the famous "Sextet"; *Don Pasquale,* an opera buffa; and *The Daughter of the Regiment* ( *La Fille du Régiment* ), a French *opéra comique.*

*Verdi.* Virtually the only Italian composer in the second half of the 19th century, Verdi was the culminating figure of Italian opera. Italian nationalism was an important ingredient in his operas, and his popularity as a national figure is attested to by the fact that his name became an acrostic symbol ( Victor Emanuelo Re D'Italia ) of the *Risorgimento* movement headed by King Victor Emmanuel II. Verdi's operas in general had greater continuity, more prominence and dramatic use of the orchestra, less stylistic distinction between recitative and aria, and certain characteristic structural traits: they were composed in four acts with choral finales to the second and third acts, and included a meditation or *preghiera* (prayer scene) opening the last act.

Verdi's six best-known operas are *Rigoletto, The Troubadour* ( *Il Trovatore* ), *The Errant Woman* ( *La Traviata* ), *Aïda,* which was commissioned for the celebration of the opening of the Suez Canal, *Otello* (libretto by Boito based on Shakespeare's *Othello*), and *Falstaff*, Verdi's last work, an opera buffa on a grand and profound scale.

**Verismo Composers.** At the end of the 19th century and the early decades of the 20th century, there was a strong current of realism in Italian opera, called *verismo opera*. Composers and works in this category were Pietro Mascagni (1863–1945), who composed *Rustic Chivalry* (*Cavalleria Rusticana*), Ruggiero Leoncavallo (1858–1919), who composed *The Clowns* (*I Pagliacci*), and Giacomo Puccini (1858–1924), whose ever-popular operas are *The Bohemian Girl* (*La Bohème*), *Tosca,* and *Madam Butterfly.*

### France

Three types of opera existed in 19th-century France; opéra comique and grand opera in the first half of the century, lyric opera in the second half.

**Opéra Comique.** The 18th-century distinction between serious and comic opera in France was retained during the first half of the 19th century. Toward the middle of the century, opéra comique began to develop in two directions: toward a more lyric and serious style on the one hand, and toward light, sentimental operettas on the other.

**Composers.** The principal composers and comic operas were François Boieldieu (1775–1834), *The White Lady* (*La Dame Blanche*); Daniel Auber (1782–1871), *Fra Diavolo;* Louis-Ferdinand Hérold (1791–1833), *The Field of Honor* (*Le Pré aux Clercs*); Victor Massé (1822–84), *The Marriage of Jeannette* (*Les Noces de Jeannette*); and Charles Gounod, *The Doctor Despite Himself* (*Le Médecin Malgré Lui*).

**Grand Opera.** In the second quarter of the 19th century, a new genre distinct from opéra comique was designated as *grand opera* or, more accurately, as *grand-spectacle opera*. It was built around grandiose plots and made use of large ensemble scenes, expanded orchestral resources, and colorful pageantry. After mid-century, these characteristics became somewhat less pronounced, and grand opera merged with comic opera.

**Composers.** The principal exponent of grand opera was Meyerbeer. His principal works were *Robert the Devil* (*Robert le Diable*), *Les Huguenots, Le Prophète,* and *L'Africaine.* Other composers and works in the same category were Auber, *The Deaf Girl of Portici* (*La Muette de Portici*); Rossini, *William Tell;* Jacques Halévy (1799–1862), *The Jewess* (*La Juive*); and Berlioz, *The Trojans* (*Les Troyens*).

**Lyric Opera.** A style-type known as *drame lyrique* (lyric drama) emerged in the second half of the 19th century. It combined the melodic appeal of opéra comique with some of the large-scale aspects of grand opera.

*Composers.* Gounod's *Faust* is a classic example of the lyric opera. Other important operas in the second half of the century were *Mignon* by Ambroise Thomas (1811–96), *Manon* and *Thaïs* by Jules Massenet (1842–1912), *Carmen* by Bizet—one of the most popular operas of all time, it was classed as an opéra comique because originally it used spoken dialogue, though there is no comic element in the work; *The King of Ys* (*Le Roi d'Ys*) by Edouard Lalo (1823–92), *Lakmé* by Léo Delibes (1836–91), *The Tales of Hoffmann* (*Les Contes d'Hoffmann*) by Jacques Offenbach (1819–80), *Samson et Dalila* by Saint-Saëns, *Louise* by Gustave Charpentier (1860–1956), *Fervaal* by Vincent d'Indy, and *Pélléas et Mélisande,* an impressionist opera by Claude Debussy.

## Germany

Germany, of secondary importance in 18th-century opera, rose to a position of eminence during the 19th century. The first half of the century was dominated by German romantic opera; the second half by Wagner's music dramas.

**Romantic Opera.** German operas borrowed much from French and Italian models, but they differed in a number of ways. (1) Subject material was drawn from medieval legends, folk tales, and fairy stories. (2) Plots leaned heavily on supernatural, mystic, and occult elements, and on wild and mysterious aspects of nature. (3) In addition to Italian-style arias, German composers employed folk tunes and melodies in folk style. (4) German romantic operas made much more use of harmonic and orchestral colors to heighten dramatic interest.

*Composers.* The central figure in German romantic opera was

Carl Maria von Weber, whose principal works were *Der Frei-schütz, Euryanthe,* and *Oberon.* Other German romantic operas were *Fidelio* by Beethoven, *Faust* and *Jessonda* by Ludwig Spohr (1784–1859), *Undine* by E. T. A. Hoffmann (1776–1822), *Hans Heiling* and *Der Vampyr* by Heinrich Marschner (1795–1861), *Genoveva* by Schumann, *Martha* by Friedrich von Flotow (1812–83), *The Merry Wives of Windsor* (*Die lustigen Weiber von Windsor*) by Otto Nicolai (1810–49), and *The Flying Dutchman* (*Der fliegende Holländer*) by Richard Wagner. *Hänsel und Gretel* by Englebert Humperdinck (1854–1921) is a popular fairy-tale opera.

**Music Drama.** German opera in the second half of the 19th century was completely dominated by the creative genius of Richard Wagner, who conceived of opera as the unification of the arts and called it *music drama.*

*Characteristics.* More than any other composer, Wagner departed from operatic tradition. (1) His concept of opera was that it should be a fusion of stagecraft, literature, and music, a conviction that led to dramatic truth and unity surpassing anything in the operatic field. (2) Wagner wrote his own libretti which, like earlier German romantic operas, employed national folklore and legend, medieval plots, supernatural elements, and themes involving redemption, often with religious implications. (3) Dramatic and musical continuity were characteristic of music dramas which abolished separate closed forms. (4) Distinction between aria and recitative was abandoned. (5) Thematic recurrence in operas had been introduced earlier, but it was Wagner who exploited the *leitmotif,* a device to enhance the drama and unify the music. Leitmotifs were themes used to represent characters, objects, situations, and emotions. (6) Wagner greatly increased the size of the orchestra, gave it a more prominent and dramatic function, and made it an important factor in the characteristic continuity of music dramas. (7) Chromatic harmony, extended modulations, nonperiodic phraseology, contrapuntal textures, and slight use of chorus are other characteristics of Wagner's music dramas.

*Works.* Wagner set forth his ideas in several treatises on the subject of music and drama: *The Artwork of the Future* and *Opera and Drama.* His early operas were *The Fairies* (*Die Feen*),

*Forbidden Love* (*Das Liebesverbot*), *Rienzi, The Flying Dutch-man* (*Der fliegende Holländer*), *Tannhäuser,* and *Lohengrin* which was the last of Wagner's romantic operas. The music dramas include an operatic tetralogy entitled *The Nibelungen Ring* (*Der Ring des Nibelungen*) containing the four operas *Das Rheingold, Die Walküre, Siegfried,* and *The Twilight of the Gods* (*Götterdämmerung*). Other music dramas were *Tristan und Isolde* and *Parsifal,* his last opera. *Die Meistersinger von Nürn-berg* is a singspiel based on the life of Hans Sachs, a famous meistersinger.

## Other National Opera ·

In addition to the most significant developments in 19th-century opera in Italy, France, and Germany, there were some outstanding operas in other countries.

**Russia.** Russian nationalism began with Glinka's *A Life for the Czar* and *Russlan and Ludmilla.* The principal Russian operas were *The Stone Guest* by Alexander Dargomizsky (1813–69), *Boris Godunov* by Mussorgsky, *Prince Igor* by Borodin, *Eugen Onegin* by Tchaikovsky, and a number of operas by Rimsky-Korsakov, including *May Night, Snow Maiden, Mlada, Sadko, The Czar's Bride, Czar Saltan, Pan Voyevoda, The Legend of the Invisible City of Kitezh,* and *The Golden Cockerel* (*Le Coq d'Or*).

**Czechoslovakia.** National Bohemian operas were the comic opera *The Bartered Bride* (*Prodaná Nevěsta*) by Smetana, and *King and Collier* and *Rusalka* by Dvořák.

**England.** The most important development in English musical theater in the 19th century were the operettas by Gilbert and Sullivan, which, because of their wit, humor, clever satire, and rollicking tunes, have remained popular. The best-known titles are *Trial by Jury, H. M. S. Pinafore, The Pirates of Penzance, Iolanthe, The Mikado, The Yeomen of the Guard,* and *The Gondoliers.*

# CHAPTER 22

*Vocal Music*

The Romantic era produced some estimable vocal literature in addition to opera. The art song was the most important type; oratorio and choral music were less important. Germany was the leading nation; France and Russia also created excellent vocal music in the late 19th century; other countries contributed relatively little of consequence.

## Art Song

The art song is a category of vocal literature distinct from popular song, folk song, and operatic aria. Its appeal to 19th-century musicians is a clear manifestation of the romantic affinity for lyric and intimate expression in concise forms.

**Characteristics.** 19th-century song composers took great pains with musical expression of the poetic text, and in no other field was there a closer tie between word and music.

*Melody.* As a vehicle for the expression of intimate poetic sentiment, vocal melody in the art song was characteristically lyric rather than dramatic. It enhanced the general mood of the poetry, and not infrequently pictorialized specific words or phrases, as shown in the excerpt from Schubert's "Alinde" (Example 24) where the phrase "The sun sank into the depths of the sea" is set to a descending melodic line, "sun" being the high point and "sea" the low point.

145

Die Son - ne sinkt___ in's tie - fe Meer

*Example 24. Musical pictorialization*

**Accompaniment.** The piano, which came into general use in the early 19th century, provided additional resources for romantic expression in the art song. The accompaniment functioned in three ways; (1) it provided harmonic and sometimes melodic support to the voice; (2) it served to punctuate the poetic form by interludes between stanzas and lines of the poem; and (3) it further enhanced the mood and meaning of the text by harmonic, rhythmic, and even melodic material independent of the voice part. For example, in Schubert's "Die Post," the sound of the posthorn as the mailcoach enters the village is suggested by a fanfare motive, and the galloping horses by the rhythm of the accompaniment.

**Form.** The musical form of a song is partly determined by poetic structure. Two basic forms are *strophic form,* in which each stanza of the poem is set to the same music, and *through-composed form,* in which the music, more closely following changing ideas and moods of the poem, is different for each stanza. *Modified strophic form* is a compromise in which the successive stanzas have modified versions of the same music. Other forms are partly strophic—some stanzas have the same music, while others are set to different music. For example, a four-stanza poem might use musical forms such as *A A B A, A B A B, A B C A,* or other plans.

**Song Cycle.** The 19th century produced a new form in the *song cycle,* a group of poems by one poet set to music by one composer. Song cycles have a central idea or mood, and usually a loosely narrative sequence of songs.

**Poets.** The art song was nourished by a flourishing romantic poetry. The poets whose names appear most frequently in 19th-century solo song literature are Johann Schiller, Heinrich Heine, Johann Goethe, Wilhelm Müller, Eduard Möricke, Joseph von Eichendorf, Wilhelm Meister, Lord George Byron (whose English poems were often translated into German), and the French symbolist poets Paul Verlaine, Stéphane Mallarmé, and Charles Baudelaire.

**Composers.** German poets and composers dominated 19th-century song literature. German lieder (songs) far outnumbered songs in other languages. The foremost lieder composers were Schubert, Schumann, Brahms, and Wolf.

*Schubert.* During his short life Schubert produced some six hundred songs. A master of melodic invention, he elevated the lied to a position of supreme artistry. His songs combined classical serenity and simplicity with romantic harmony and lyric melody. Generally he favored strophic and modified strophic forms as in "The Wanderer" ("Das Wandern"), and "Thou Art Repose" ("Du bist die Ruh"), respectively. His two song cycles, *The Maid of the Mill* (*Die Schöne Müllerin*) and *Winter Journey* (*Winterreise*) are masterpieces in that form and contain some of Schubert's most beautiful songs.

*Schumann.* Schumann's songs are romantic in every sense. An outstanding characteristic is the prominence of the piano which at times outweighs the voice part. Piano introductions, interludes, and postludes are frequently long. Two song cycles are *Woman's Love and Life* (*Frauenliebe und Leben*) and *Poet's Love* (*Dichterliebe*).

*Brahms.* Like Schubert, Brahms preferred strophic form, and his songs lean toward a folk style, less highly charged with emotion than those of Schumann. He composed more than 260 songs, the *Magelone* song cycle, and *Four Serious Songs* (*Vier Ernste Gesänge*) composed on biblical texts.

*Wolf.* Hugo Wolf (1860–1903) was a specialist in lieder. His flexible and nonperiodic phraseology and frequent chromaticism reflect influence of Wagner, whom he emulated. His 250 lieder were mostly in through-composed form. He is noted for subtlety of musical expression. Though he composed no song cycles, he concentrated on one poet at a time (Eichendorff, Goethe, Mörike). In addition are the collections of songs on texts translated from Spanish poems (*Spanisches Liederbuch*) and Italian poems *Italienisches Liederbuch*).

*Other Lieder Composers.* Other German composers who contributed to 19th-century song literature were Beethoven, whose song cycle was entitled *To the Distant Beloved* (*An die Ferne*

*Geliebte*), Karl Loewe (1796–1869), who was a master of the strophic ballad form, Mendelssohn, Robert Franz (1815–92), Peter Cornelius (1824–74), and Richard Strauss.

**French Art Song.** The poems of Baudelaire, Mallarmé, and Verlaine were the chief inspiration for an excellent but limited French song literature which flourished in the second half of the century. The principal composers were Gounod, Fauré (song cycle: *La Bonne Chanson*), Ernest Chausson (1855–99), Henri Duparc (1848–1933), and Claude Debussy (song cycle: *Chansons de Bilitis.*)

**Russian Composers.** Late 19th-century Russian composers, better known for their contributions to other categories of music, produced some notable song literature. The most important of these were Tchaikovsky, Rachmaninoff, Alexander Gretchaninov (1864–1956), Reinhold Glière (1875–1956), and Mussorgsky, who composed two fine song cycles: *Sunless* and *Songs and Dances of Death.*

## Oratorio

Oratorio did not attract romantic composers to the extent that opera and solo song did. To the Handelian concept, which continued to dominate oratorio in the 19th century, were added romantic subjectivity and expanded orchestral resources.

Felix Mendelssohn was the most eminent composer of 19th-century oratorio, chiefly because of his mastery of choral technique. His fame in this field rests on two masterpieces: *St. Paul* and *Elijah.* Other notable oratorios of the century were Beethoven's *Christ on the Mount of Olives*, Spohr's *The Last Judgement*, Schumann's *Paradise and the Peri*, Berlioz's *The Childhood of Christ*, Liszt's *Legend of St. Elizabeth* and *Christus*, Franck's *The Beatitudes*, Brahms's *A German Requiem*, which employs a biblical rather than liturgical text, Stainer's *The Crucifixion*, Parry's *Judith*, *Job*, and *King Saul*, and Elgar's *The Dream of Gerontius.*

## Other Religious Choral Music

The Romantic era was not one of the great periods in church music. The distinction between true oratorio and other religious music rested mainly on textual rather than formal and stylistic considerations. Psalms and other liturgical texts were set to music more often as festival works for concert performance than as functional church music. Like oratorio, romantic church music made use of large choruses, solo voices, and orchestra, but unlike oratorio it did not employ narrator and recitative.

The principal composers of Masses and other music on Catholic liturgical texts were Beethoven (*Missa Solemnis*), Cherubini, Schubert, Rossini (*Stabat Mater*), Mendelssohn (*Psalms* and *Lauda Sion*), Brahms (*Motets* for female chorus, op. 29, 74, and 110), Berlioz (*Requiem* and *Te Deum*), Liszt (*Graner Mass* and *Hungarian Coronation Mass*), Verdi (*Requiem*), Gounod (*St. Cecelia Mass*), Franck (*Psalms*), Fauré (*Requiem*), and Bruckner. Mention should also be made of the Russian Dimitri Bortniansky (1751–1825), who composed religious choral works for the Greek Orthodox Church.

## Secular Choral Music

The rise of nationalism and interest in folk song provided impetus for secular choral music as did also the formation of numerous choral groups and societies. Choral media ranged from unaccompanied part songs to cantata-like works with solo voices and orchestra. Choral media were also employed in a number of symphonic works (Beethoven, Listz, Mahler, and others).

Mendelssohn, one of the foremost composers of romantic choral music of all kinds, wrote some fifty unaccompanied part songs and *Walpurgisnacht,* a secular cantata. Matching Mendelssohn's excellence in choral media, Brahms wrote numerous works for men's, women's, and mixed choruses, unaccompanied and with various accompanying media. Among his principal works are the *Rhapsody* for contralto, male chorus, and orchestra, *Song of Destiny, Song of Triumph, Nänie,* and the *Liebeslieder Waltzes* for mixed chorus (or four solo voices) with four-hand piano accompaniment. Other secular choral works are Berlioz's *The Damnation of Faust* and Schumann's *Scenes from Goethe's Faust.*

# CHAPTER 23

# Instrumental Music

Individualism, nationalism, program music, and virtuosity were especially prominent traits in instrumental music. Short piano miniatures and lengthy symphonic works were manifestations of romantic extremes. The piano and orchestra were the principal media; chamber music was less important.

## Keyboard Music

The piano was to instrumental media what the art song was to vocal music. Attracting composer and performer alike, it was one of the most important media in all 19th-century music. Organ music was of negligible importance.

**The Piano.** Because of its capacity for sonority, dynamic range, and gradations between loud and soft—characteristics which the harpsichord lacked—the piano was the romantic instrument par excellence. Not only was it the leading solo instrument but it was an important ingredient in chamber ensembles. It provided composer and performer with possibilities of emotional expression ranging from the intimate to the grandiose, and from delicate lyricism to bombastic showiness. The damper pedal enabled composers to experiment with new harmonic effects, and the improved keyboard mechanism was a stimulant to new idioms, techniques, and virtuosity. (See Figure 10, page 102.)

**Forms.** As in other media, 19th-century piano composers were less concerned with musical form than with content and subjective expression.

*Sonata.* After Beethoven and Schubert, the piano sonata attracted few composers, and classical sonata form was largely abandoned in favor of single-movement pieces.

*Dances.* Stylized dances constituted a large portion of romantic piano literature. The most common were the waltz, Ländler (an Austrian waltz in slow tempo), mazurka, polonaise, ecossaise, polka, galop, and other national dances.

*Etude.* The *etude*, basically a study featuring some technical aspect of performance (e.g., scales, arpeggios, figurations, octaves, chords), was composed as a virtuoso piece for concert audiences.

*Character Pieces.* Short pieces conveying a general mood and those most specifically programmatic with descriptive titles are classified as *character pieces*. They include compositions with such titles as arabesque, ballade, intermezzo, nocturne, romanza, lament, moment musicale, rhapsody, impromptu, bagatelle, songs without words, and descriptive titles such as "Butterflies," "Colored Leaves," and many more.

*Variations.* After Beethoven, piano variations were largely shallow virtuoso show pieces. The variation form was of little consequence in romantic piano music.

**Composers.** The most extensive piano literature in the 19th century was composed by Germans.

*Beethoven.* Nineteenth-century piano literature began with Beethoven's monumental sonatas and variations, which were seldom emulated by romantic composers.

*Schubert.* Schubert's piano style fused classical form and reserve with romantic lyricism and expression. His piano music includes eleven sonatas, six impromptus, eight moments musicales, some piano duets, but no concertos or programmatic works.

*Mendelssohn.* In addition two piano concertos and some preludes and fugues reflecting his admiration for Bach, Mendelssohn's principal piano works were some fifty romantic pieces called *Songs without Words* (*Lieder ohne Worte*), many of which were published with descriptive titles added by the publishers, such as the famous "Spinning Song."

*Schumann.* Until about 1840, Schumann devoted himself almost exclusively to piano composition. His works consist mainly of short character pieces with descriptive titles grouped in collections entitled *Butterflies* (*Papillons*), *Scenes of Childhood*

(*Kinderscenen*), *Carnaval*, *Fantasy Pieces* (*Fantasiestücke*), and others.

**Chopin.** The most illustrious composer of piano music in the century, Chopin was a specialist in that medium and composed little else. His music is eminently idiomatic, revealing his keen sense of properties and capacities of the piano. He used no descriptive titles, and wrote mostly single-movement works. Outstanding characteristics are strictly homophonic texture, extensive chromaticism and modulation, superb melodic and harmonic ingenuity, limited virtuosity, and general refinement and delicacy of style. His compositions include nocturnes, scherzi, twenty-four preludes in all major and minor keys, waltzes, stylized Polish dances (polonaises and mazurkas), twenty-seven etudes, impromptus, three sonatas, and two piano concertos.

**Liszt.** Liszt was the foremost pianist-composer of the 19th century. His piano compositions generally fall in three categories: brilliant virtuoso compositions, pieces with quiet romantic lyricism, and transcriptions of opera arias, lieder, symphonies, and Bach's organ fugues. His principal works are the *Hungarian Rhapsodies,* two piano concertos, twelve brilliant etudes entitled *Transcendental Etudes* (*Etudes d'exécution transcendante*), three sets of short poetic pieces entitled *Years of Pilgrimage* (*Années de Pélerinage*), and the *Petrarch Sonnets.*

**Brahms.** Brahms's music, though romantic in melody, harmony, texture and sonority, is nevertheless classically inclined in the sense of absolute forms and formal details, avoidance of programmatic or literary allusions, and absence of showy virtuosity. Character pieces include ballades, rhapsodies, capriccios, and intermezzi. He wrote three piano sonatas and several sets of variations, including *Variations on a Theme of Haydn* for two pianos.

**Other Composers.** Enormous quantities of inferior piano music were turned out by second-rate composers in the early part of the century. They include names now mostly forgotten: Johann Hummel, Adolf von Henselt, Friedrich Kalkbrenner, Sigismond Thalberg, and others. The sonatas and etudes, such as *Steps to Parnassus* (*Gradus ad Parnassum*) by Muzio Clementi (1752–1832), and the music of John Field were noteworthy contributions to piano literature. Other composers were the German Max Reger (1873–1916), the Norwegian Edvard Grieg, the American Edward MacDowell (1861–1908), the Frenchmen Gabriel Fauré and César Franck, the Spaniards Isaac Albéniz and Enrique Granados, the Italian Ferruccio Busoni (1866–1924), the Russians Mussorgsky, Anton Rubinstein (1829–94), and Sergei Rachmaninoff, who was the last of the romantic pianist-composers.

**Organ Music.** After Bach, the organ was neglected during the classical and most of the romantic periods. The most important developments took place in the late 19th century and mainly in France. Principal composers were Mendelssohn, Liszt, Franck, Reger, and Charles Widor (1844–1937).

## Symphonic Music

The orchestra, one of the great media of the romantic era, expanded in size, resources for color, and range of sonorities.

**Instrumentation.** Each of the four choirs added instruments beyond those of the classical orchestra.

*Woodwinds.* More than two each of flutes, oboes, clarinets, and bassoons were used. Additional woodwinds were piccolo, bass clarinet, English horn, and contrabassoon.

*Brass.* The brass choir usually included four horns which, along with trumpets, trombones, and tubas, gave tremendous power and sonority to the orchestra. The advent of valves gave more versatility and melodic potential to brass instruments.

*Percussion.* To the classical timpani were added many percussion instruments: bass and side drums and a large assortment of "color" instruments such as the harp, triangle, castanets, gongs, cymbals, chimes, bells, xylophones, and celestas.

*Strings.* No new instruments were added to the string choir, but it expanded in numbers to balance the larger woodwind and brass choirs. Unlike classical scores, the string parts were written on five staves.

**Orchestration.** Composers sought new effects for expressive purposes. There was more use of solo passages, especially for individual woodwind instruments and horn. Special string effects were used: pizzicato, double stopping, mutes, tremolo, harmonics, and others. The composers who contributed most notably to the technique of orchestration were Berlioz, Liszt, Wagner (in opera), and Rimsky-Korsakov, at the end of the century.

**Forms.** New concepts in symphonic forms were added to the basic classical symphony and concerto forms.

*Symphony.* Works entitled "Symphony" were composed by most of the major romantic composers. Only in the broadest outlines did they follow the precepts of the classical symphony. They varied the number of movements, used more contrasting keys in the inner movements, used freer forms for internal structure of movements, and generally made the symphony a vehicle for expression rather than a formal design. In a number of instances composers added chorus and solo voices to the orchestra (Beethoven, Berlioz, Liszt, Mahler, and others). The program symphony was an important romantic development.

*Concerto.* The piano and violin were the chief solo instruments employed in the concerto. Generally it was a brilliant show piece for the virtuoso soloist. The romantic concerto retained the classical three-movement plan.

*Symphonic Poem.* A new symphonic form, called *symphonic poem* or *tone poem,* was introduced by Franz Liszt around the middle of the century. It is a one-movement programmatic work with descriptive title and based on some literary work or legend. Some famous symphonic poems are *Les Préludes* by Liszt, *The Moldau* (the second of six symphonic poems collectively entitled *My Fatherland*) by Smetana, *Night on Bald Mountain* by Mussorgsky, *The Sorcerer's Apprentice* by Dukas, *Danse Macabre* by Saint-Saëns, *On the Steppes of Central Asia* by Borodin, *Finlandia* by Sibelius, *Prelude to the Afternoon of a Faun* (*Prélude à l'Après-midi d'un Faune*) by Debussy, *Isle of the Dead* by Rachmaninoff, and *Till Eulenspiegel* by Richard Strauss.

*Concert Overture.* Single-movement works, called *concert overtures,* were usually in sonata-allegro form but were not orchestral introductions to operas. To some extent they were programmatic and often had descriptive titles. Examples are Mendelssohn's *Fingal's Cave Overture,* Brahms's *Academic Festival Overture,* and Tchaikovsky's *1812 Overture.*

*Symphonic Variations.* Relatively few orchestral works were in variation form. Some notable examples are Brahms's *Variations on a Theme of Haydn,* Franck's *Symphonic Variations* for piano solo and orchestra, d'Indy's *Istar Variations,* and Elgar's *Enigma Variations.*

*Symphonic Suite.* Symphonic suites are programmatic works in several movements which do not follow symphonic form. In this category are originally composed fantasies such as Rimsky-Korsakov's *Scheherazade,* arrangements of ballet music such as Tchaikovsky's *Nutcracker Suite,* and incidental music to plays such as Mendelssohn's *Midsummer Night's Dream* and Grieg's *Peer Gynt Suite.*

*Dances.* Semipopular orchestral music in dance forms includes the Johann Strauss waltzes and other dances by a number of composers.

**Composers.** Germans led the field in symphonic composition. As nationalism became a strong current after about 1850, more composers in other countries contributed to the literature.

*Beethoven.* Beethoven's nine symphonies are the beginning of the expansion of symphonic form and medium. His Sixth Symphony (the *Pastoral Symphony*) in five movements was the first program symphony. The finale of his Ninth Symphony contains the first use of solo voices and chorus in a symphony.

*Schubert.* Schubert wrote eight symphonies in classical orchestral medium and form. Romantic elements in his music are the lyrical melodies and ingenious harmonies. Best known are the "Unfinished" Symphony in B Minor and the C Minor Symphony.

*Mendelssohn.* The best of Mendelssohn's five symphonies are the last three, popularly known as the *Scotch, Italian,* and *Reformation.* They are in classical four-movement form with refined romantic materials. Other symphonic works are the incidental music to Shakespeare's *Midsummer Night's Dream,* which contains the famous "Overture," "Scherzo," and "Wedding March," two piano concertos, the *Violin Concerto in E Minor,* and the concert overtures *Fingal's Cave* (also called *Hebrides Overture*), *Calm Sea and Prosperous Voyage,* and *Melusine.*

*Schumann.* Schumann's symphonic music is less programmatic than Mendelssohn's, and his orchestration less colorful. He composed four symphonies, a piano concerto, violin concerto, and cello concerto.

*Berlioz.* The most programmatic symphonic music in the first half of the century and the greatest advances in romantic orchestration are attributed to Berlioz. He wrote the first treatise on orchestration. He employed *cyclical form* (the recurrence of one or more themes in successive movements), and *idée fixe* (a symphonic leitmotif representing a character). His principal symphonic work is the five-movement programmatic *Fantastic Symphony*. Other works are *Harold in Italy* (based on Byron's *Childe Harold*), *Romeo and Juliet* for orchestra, solo voices, and chorus, and *Roman Carnival Overture*.

**Liszt.** Liszt's main contributions are thirteen symphonic poems, two program symphonies (*Faust Symphony* in three movements entitled "Faust," "Gretchen," and "Mephistopheles," the finale of which employs a male chorus, and *Dante Symphony* in two movements), and two brilliant virtuoso piano concertos, in E Flat and A Major.

**Brahms.** Brahms's four symphonies are thoroughly romantic in style but are not programmatic. They follow expanded classical form. Other symphonic works include two piano concertos, one violin concerto, a double concerto for violin and cello, *Variations on a Theme of Haydn, Academic Festival Overture,* and *Tragic Overture.*

**Bruckner.** Bruckner's ten symphonies (the last incomplete) are notable for their great length and gigantic orchestras. They are absolute music and all are in four movements. He composed no concertos or other symphonic forms.

**Mahler.** Like Bruckner, Mahler wrote ten symphonies, the last unfinished. His second, third, fourth, and eighth symphonies make use of voices. The Eighth Symphony, appropriately known as *The Symphony of a Thousand,* represents the ultimate in gigantic form and medium. It calls for an enormous orchestra, a band, two mixed choruses, a boys' choir, and seven solo voices. Mahler composed a song cycle for solo voices and orchestra, entitled *Song of the Earth.*

**Tchaikovksy.** The last three of Tchaikovsky's six symphonies are the best known. Other symphonic works are the symphonic poems *Romeo and Juliet* (called an "Overture Fantasy") and *Francesca da Rimini,* the *1812 Overture,* three piano concertos, a violin concerto, and a *Serenade in C* for string orchestra.

**Smetana.** Smetana was a Czech nationalist known chiefly for his six "musical landscapes" entitled *My Fatherland (Má Vlast).*

**Dvořák.** One of the prolific symphonic composers in the late 19th century was Dvořák. The most famous of his nine symphonies is No. 5, *Symphony from the New World.* He composed symphonic variations, six concert overtures, five symphonic poems, three *Slavonic Rhapsodies,* a violin concerto, piano concerto, and two cello concertos.

*Franck.* The French school of romantic symphonic music began with César Franck. He composed one symphony, in D Minor, *Symphonic Variations* with piano solo, and the symphonic poems *Les Éolides, Le Chausseur Maudit, Les Djinns* for piano and orchestra, and *Psyché* for chorus and orchestra.

*Saint-Saëns.* Saint-Saëns wrote symphonies (the third with organ and piano four hands), concertos, and the ever-popular tone poem *Danse Macabre.*

*D'Indy.* D'Indy wrote three symphonies, the best known of which is the *Symphony on a French Mountain Air* for piano and orchestra, and the *Istar Variations.*

*Strauss.* Richard Strauss composed most of his symphonic poems in the 1890s. His orchestration and other aspects of style foreshadow modern techniques, though his music remains essentially romantic. His principal symphonic poems are *Aus Italian, Death and Transfiguration (Tod und Verklärung), Till Eulenspiegel, Thus Spake Zarathustra, Don Quixote, A Hero's Life (Ein Heldenleben).* Two program symphonies are *The Domestic Symphony* and *An Alpine Symphony.*

*Sibelius.* Though he lived past the middle of the 20th century, Jean Sibelius belongs mainly to the romantic tradition. He was Finland's greatest composer. His field was principally symphonic music. He composed seven symphonies and symphonic poems, the best known of which are *Finlandia, En Saga, Swan of Tuonela, Tapiola,* and *Pohjola's Daugher.* His *Karelia Suite,* like his symphonic poems, is based on Finnish legends.

*Rachmaninoff.* Like Sibelius, Rachmaninoff belongs to the romantic period though he lived until 1943. His symphonic works include two symphonies, four piano concertos, the symphonic poem *Isle of the Dead,* and symphonic variations for piano and orchestra entitled *Rhapsody on a Theme of Paganini.*

## Chamber Music

Chamber music was one of the least favored media among 19th-century composers, mainly because it lacks the intimacy of the piano on the one hand and the massive, colorful, and emotional capacities of the orchestra on the other. No program music was written for chamber ensembles.

**Media.** The string quartet continued to be the most favored chamber medium. There was an appreciable increase in the number of chamber works employing the piano in trios, quartets, and quintets. Solo sonatas for violin and other instruments were relatively few.

**Composers.** After Beethoven and Schubert, the foremost contributions to chamber music were those of Brahms and Dvořák. Composers who contributed most to chamber music literature were mainly those who had classical leanings.

*Beethoven.* Nineteenth-century chamber music, like piano and symphonic music, began with Beethoven. His output in chamber music included sixteen string quartets, four string trios, six piano trios, ten violin sonatas, five cello sonatas, a horn sonata, and a quintet for piano and wind instruments.

*Schubert.* Among Schubert's fifteen string quartets, the best known is the Quartet in D Minor, known as *Death and the Maiden* because the andantino movement is a set of variations on Schubert's song of the same title. Another well-known work is the *Trout Quintet,* which also includes a set of variations for the slow movement on Schubert's song "Die Forelle."

*Mendelssohn.* Mendelssohn's chamber music includes six string quartets, two quintets, an octet, a sextet for piano and strings, two piano trios, one violin sonata, and two cello sonatas.

*Schumann.* Schumann composed three string quartets, three piano trios, a piano quartet, a piano quintet, solo sonatas, and other works for various combinations of instruments.

*Brahms.* Brahms, the "romantic classicist," composed some twenty-four works in this category, including string quartets, quintets, sextets, a clarinet quintet, a piano quintet, piano quartets, piano trios, a trio for clarinet, cello and piano, the famous *Horn Trio* for violin, piano, and French horn, and sonatas for piano and various solo instruments.

*Dvořák.* Dvořák was the most important chamber composer at the end of the century. His works include thirteen string quartets, two string quintets, one sextet, two piano quartets, four piano trios, one string trio, and one piano quintet.

*Franck.* Franck wrote a string quartet, piano quintet, four piano trios, and the Violin Sonata in A Major, his most popular chamber work.

*Fauré.* Fauré's chamber music includes two piano quartets, two piano quintets, a piano trio, a string quartet, two violin sonatas, and two cello sonatas.

# VII

*The*
*Twentieth*
*Century*

# CHAPTER 24

# General Considerations

The 20th century has witnessed changes which in frequency and magnitude are unmatched in any previous history.

**Historical Background.** Events and developments in political, social, scientific, and cultural history have inevitably and profoundly influenced the course of music history since 1900.

*Political Events.* Two global wars in the first half of the century had powerful impacts on world history: World War I (1914–18) and World War II (1939–45). Each conflict was followed by an effort to establish world government: the League of Nations (1920–46) and the United Nations (established in 1946). The Bolshevik Revolution in 1917 marked the emergence of Communism and of Russia as a world power. After World War II Japan and China also became major world powers. Notable conflicts since mid-century were the Korean War (1950–53), the Arab-Israeli conflict, and the Vietnamese wars involving first France and later the United States. Political and ideological struggle between Russia and the United States since World War II is known as the Cold War, a period of nonmilitary activity, but one marked by a major armaments race.

*Social and Economic Developments.* Of great significance has been the decline of colonialism and the rise of independent states, especially in Africa and India. Greater autonomy was granted British Commonwealth countries, notably Canada, Australia, and New Zealand. Mention should be made of the economic depression in the 1930s and the European Common Market since World War II.

Since about 1960 a number of acute social and economic problems have arisen or grown more acute: tremendous acceleration in population growth; racial and student unrest resulting in demonstrations and riots; rise of crime, violence, and illegal use of narcotics; environmental pollution; monetary inflation; urban decay; and severe poverty and food shortages in many parts of the world.

*Technology.* Tremendous advances in science and engineering and their application to industry have affected social, economic, and cultural history. Far-reaching developments have taken place in biology, chemistry, physics (nuclear, electronic, and acoustical branches), and astronomy. Technology has made astounding progress in the fields of communication, transportation, and medicine.

Some specific innovations are radio, television, atomic energy in military and industrial uses, transistors, the laser beam, jet propulsion, digital computers and data processing, antibiotics, photo duplication, exploration of outer space (which produced the first landing on the moon by Apollo 11 astronauts in 1969), exploration of suboceanic areas, and, especially relevant to music, high-fidelity sound transmission.

*The Fine Arts.* As in all past history, the spirit of the times is reflected in the fine arts. General 20th-century traits are frequency and rapidity of change, experimentation with new forms and media, and mixed media. In the visual arts a general trend away from realism and toward abstract and nonobjective expression may be noted. Distinctly new visual media are the cinema and still photography. Proliferation of "isms" in art since 1900 precludes anything more than mention of some of the important trends and artists in this summary: expressionism (also in drama and music), cubism (Picasso, Braque), surrealism (Dali, Chagall), dadaism (Duchamp), abstract expressionism (Pollock), geometric abstractionism (Stella), neoplasticism (Mondrian). Further developments are in mixed media, kinetic (moving) art, temporal (or momentary) art, pop art (commonplace realism), op art (optical illusion), minimal art, and conceptual art. Perhaps the most significant developments in architecture stem from the establishment of the Bauhaus.

Developments in literature, poetry, and theatre have kept apace with those in the other fine arts. Social protest, existentialism (Sartre), pessimism and despair, absurdity, and intentional "shock value," including obscenity and brutality, are some of the more pronounced traits.

**Problems in 20th-Century Music History.** The study of 20th-century music from the historical point of view poses a number of special problems not encountered in earlier periods.

*Terminology.* No satisfactory designation, comparable to Renaissance or Baroque has yet been devised for 20th-century music. "Modern music" is commonly used, but its connotations are so variable as to be nearly meaningless, for it can mean all 20th-century music or else only that which is revolutionary in some respect as opposed to romantic music. "New music" (comparable to *Ars Nova* in the 14th century and *nuove musiche* in the early 17th century) has been suggested but is unsatisfactory because it limits the literature mainly to avant-garde developments, and because music of the early 1900s is no longer "new." The expression "contemporary period" is likewise misleading because it connotes that which is currently in vogue, and what is going on today is quite unlike that which was being heard in the early decades of the century.

*Historical Perspective.* Whereas we can view each past era more or less as a whole, we are too close to the 20th century to acquire such perspective. We cannot grasp modern music objectively because it is still in the present; hence we cannot evaluate it unequivocally.

*Quantity of Music.* Because of the enormous amount of music composed since 1900, no one can possibly be familiar with more than a small fraction of the literature. Even the quantity of music composed in the 19th century is small by comparison.

*Diversity.* The diversity of trends, styles, and techniques which have been evident since 1900 preclude the possibility of studying the music as one coordinated whole. No single trend represents the century or even a substantial portion of it. Furthermore, in time sequence these developments overlap in bewildering fashion.

*Rapidity of Change.* It may be noted that generally each successive period in music history has become shorter. The 20th century, in music as in other aspects of modern culture, is especially noted for acceleration in frequency and rapidity of change. Some innovations have emerged and expired within a decade.

*Complexity.* Twentieth-century music has become far more complex in terms of melody, harmony, tonality, rhythm, texture, and form. These elements combine virtually to preclude the kind of systematic analysis which can be applied to the music of earlier periods.

*Transmission.* The means of musical transmission have expanded enormously. In addition to vast resources for live concert performance, music is also communicated to a large public by new acoustical means: radio, television, cinema, public address systems, disc and tape recording. The modern individual is confronted with an almost constant bombardment of musical sounds of all types and qualities, making critical judgment far more difficult to exercise.

**Commercial and Academic Aspects.** In addition to creative and aesthetic considerations, music has undergone a number of significant new developments.

*Commercial Aspects.* Music has become big business, supported by a large body of consumers. Important commercially sponsored enterprises are public concerts by professional artists and organizations (symphony orchestras, opera companies, choruses, and chamber ensembles). Companies manufacturing musical instruments, radios, phonographs, and tape recorders are an integral part of the musical scene. Publication of books, periodicals, and musical scores has disseminated music and musical information to a degree unknown in the past. The recording industry, too, has made available a vast literature representing music of the past and present.

*Education.* Prior to 1900, music education was almost entirely limited to training professional performers and composers by private instruction in conservatories. Today music is part of virtually all education at all levels. In higher education it includes the areas of performance, composition, theory, history and literature, musicology, and teacher training. Furthermore, it holds a prominent place as a liberal arts subject for nonprofessionals.

*Musicology.* Scholarly research in all aspects of music, but especially in music history, has made tremendous strides since its inception in the 19th century. Manifestations of the growing interest in this discipline are: (1) the impressive number of anthologies and complete works of individual composers now published in modern score and available in libraries, (2) the number of scholarly periodicals and books in music, (3) the fact that musicology is a universally recognized discipline in higher education, and (4) the increasing number of distinguished musicologists.

*Ethnomusicology,* concerned mainly with the music of non-European systems, has gained momentum. Recording and studying the folk music of cultures all over the world has become a major interest reflected by the books, periodicals, and commercial recordings in the field of ethnic music.

# CHAPTER 25

# General Trends in Music

A number of general trends substantiate the characteristic diversity of music since 1900. They do not form a neat chronological sequence; rather, they are overlapping developments, some of longer duration than others, some more prominent and pervasive than others. Furthermore, they are neither distinctly nor consistently separate developments. More than one trend is often absorbed in the individual style of a single composer.

**Romanticism.** While radical innovations were emerging in the early decades, romantic currents remained dominant. Subjectivity, emotionalism, programmatic bases, and large orchestras were some of the traits which persisted even in compositions which employed new harmonies, rhythms, timbres, and tonalities. Composers who belong to the post-romantic tradition (most of whom have already been mentioned in the preceding chapters on the romantic period) are Stanford and Elgar in England, Mahler and Richard Strauss in Germany, Sibelius in Finland, Grieg in Norway, Glière, Alexander Glazunov (1865–1936), and Rachmaninoff in Russia, Mascagni, Leoncavallo, and Puccini in Italy, Manuel de Falla (1876–1946) in Spain, Saint-Saëns and Fauré in France, Leoš Janáček (1854–1928) in Czechoslovakia, and MacDowell in America.

**Impressionism.** The first important trend toward 20th-century modernism in music was impressionism. In the hands of Claude Debussy, it paralleled movements in French painting, sculpture, and poetry. Largely a reaction against German romanticism, it developed new styles and techniques.

*Style.* Although impressionistic music was romantically sub-jective and programmatic, it departed from 19th-century prac-tices in a number of ways. It may be described generally as hav-ing a high degree of refinement, delicacy, vagueness of form, and a sort of "luminous fog" atmosphere. More specific characteristics are (1) neomodality, (2) open chords (fifths and octaves with-out thirds), (3) prominence of ninth chords and some new chord structures, (4) parallelism and other unorthodox chord progres-sions, (5) use of the whole-tone scale (six whole steps to the octave), (6) free rhythms and less prominence of bar-line regularity, and (7) wide spacing and extreme registers, espe-cially in piano music.

*Composers.* In addition to Debussy, composers who employed impressionist techniques were Maurice Ravel (1875–1937) in France, Frederick Delius (1862–1934) in England, de Falla in Spain, Ottorino Respighi (1879–1936) in Italy, Alexander Scriabin (1872–1915) in Russia, Selim Palmgren (1878–1951) in Finland, and Charles Loeffler (1861–1935) and Charles Griffes (1884–1920) in America.

**Expressionism.** Expressionism, another term borrowed from the visual arts (see page 164), was a less significant movement in music. From about 1910 to 1930 it was partly a German reac-tion to French impressionism. It sought to express the subcon-scious. Being emotionally oriented music, it retained a certain degree of romanticism. The style is harshly dissonant and atonal. Two names most closely identified with expressionism are Arnold Schoenberg (1874–1951, *Pierrot Lunaire*) and Alban Berg (1885–1935, *Wozzeck*).

**Neoclassicism.** Neoclassicism is a very extensive and pervasive trend. Beginning about 1920, it continues to be a dominant trend today. In a general sense it implies a return to pre-romantic ideals of objectivity and clarity of texture, but it is not confined to 18th-century classicism. The new classicism also includes the revival of contrapuntal textures and forms (fugue, passacaglia, toccata, madrigal) from the Renaissance and Baroque while employing modern harmony, rhythm, tonality, melody, and timbres.

*Composers.* Although a majority of composers have incorpo-rated some neoclassical elements in their music, the principal representatives and some examples are Igor Stravinsky (1822–1971, *Octet for Winds* and *L'Histoire du Soldat*); Sergei Prokofiev

(1891–1953, *Classical Symphony*); Paul Hindemith (1895–1963, *Ludus Tonalis* for piano, and *Fourth String Quartet*); and Anton Webern (1883–1945, transparent textures and dissonant counterpoint, *Cantatas*, Op. 29 and 31).

**Gebrauchsmusik.** Originating with Hindemith in the 1920s, *Gebrauchsmusik* (freely translated as "functional music" or "everyday music") was an offshoot of neoclassicism. It was music intended primarily for amateur performance, specified occasions, or informal gatherings. Attempting to lessen the gap between composer on the one hand and performer and listener on the other, it avoided technical difficulties and although in modern idiom was less extreme than the avant-garde music of the time. Gebrauchsmusik was never a widespread movement and it has long since been absorbed in other trends. Representative works in this category are Hindemith's *Plöner Musiktag*, composed for an amateur music festival in Plöner, *Let's Build a City* (*Wir bauen eine Stadt*), and *Funeral Music* (*Trauermusik*), composed on the occasion of the death of King George V of England in 1936.

**Jazz.** Distinctly a 20th-century phenomenon and essentially a popular American art, jazz is a significant category which has influenced all branches of serious composition.

*Definition.* Jazz has no standard definition. Some authorities limit the term to improvised instrumental dance music ("hot jazz" or "pure jazz"); to others it means almost any form of popular music. In the following summary it will be used in the broader sense, but excludes most popular song types, neofolk songs, hit tunes, and "protest" songs, all of which nevertheless often form the basis of jazz improvisations.

*Ragtime.* Ragtime probably originated in the minstrel shows in the late 19th century. It lasted from the turn of the century to the end of World War I. Ragtime was essentially music for piano solo, but the style was also used in early dance bands. Its most prominent traits were (1) persistent syncopation over an "umpah" accompaniment (alternating octaves and chords in the left hand) and (2) strains (period forms) of eight, sixteen, and thirty-two bars. Classic examples are Scott Joplin's "Maple Leaf Rag" and Zez Confrey's "Kitten on the Keys."

*Blues.* A style known as *blues*, which probably originated in work songs and Negro spirituals in the American South, was prominent during the first three decades. It was a type of solo song which soon permeated jazz bands. Blues songs dealt with melancholy subjects, self-pity, the lost lover, and the like. Blues style is characterized by twelve-bar periods (three four-measure phrases), lowered third and seventh scale degrees, and "bending" (slurring) melodic tones upward or downward from the normal pitch. Famous blues singers were "Ma" Rainey, Bessie Smith, and Ethel Waters. Examples of blues in song and band are Jelly Roll Morton's "Jelly Roll Blues," W. C. Handy's "Memphis Blues," and, most famous of all, "St. Louis Blues."

**Dixieland Jazz.** Concurrent with ragtime and blues was Dixieland jazz, a dance-band style which first centered around New Orleans. At first it was music played by black people in the form of lively marches for processions leaving the cemetery after funerals, or for dancing and entertainment in the "pleasure houses" (bordellos) in the famous Storeyville district of New Orleans. Dixieland bands usually consisted of a cornet, trombone, clarinet, banjo and drums. The musicians, most of whom could not read musical scores, improvised on a given tune such as "When the Saints Come Marching In" and "Oh Didn't He Ramble." In the 1920s the center of jazz activity shifted from New Orleans to Chicago, where piano, tuba, and tenor saxophone were added, guitar replaced banjo, and Caucasian musicians entered the field. Names associated with these bands were Buddy Bolden, Scott Joplin, King Oliver, Louis Armstrong, Bix Beiderbecke, and Bunk Johnson.

**Rise of Big Bands.** A trend toward larger bands began in the 1920s and continued through the next decade. These bands relied on written arrangements of popular tunes rather than on improvisation. They provided concert entertainment as well as ballroom dance music. A notable event in 1924 was the performance, in New York's Aeolian Hall, of George Gershwin's *Rhapsody in Blue* by the Paul Whiteman Band, a landmark in the history of jazz because it combined composition with jazz styles. Also toward the end of the 1920s, a new style of singing, called *crooning,* had a popular vogue, with vocalists (Rudy Vallee, Bing Crosby) who sang and recorded with name bands.

**Swing.** *Swing* dominated the 1930s. The standard ensemble consisted of independent sections, usually four each, of trumpets, trombones, saxophones, and a rhythm section. Arrangements fixed the basic harmonic and melodic elements but allowed latitude for melodic and rhythmic improvisation in solo sections. Some of the prominent name bands were directed by Fletcher Henderson, Duke Ellington, Benny Goodman, Jimmy Dorsey, Harry James, Guy Lombardo, Stan Kenton, Count Basie, Woody Herman, and Glenn Miller. Each band developed its own distinctive style.

*Boogie-Woogie.* Concurrent with swing was a piano solo style, known as *boogie-woogie,* which consisted of an ostinato figure in the left hand over which melodic and harmonic material was improvised.

*Bop.* A style known as *bop, bebop,* or *rebop* was the main current in the 1940s. It was characterized by a return to smaller ensembles (called "combos"), including amplified guitar, faster tempo, improvised melody over fixed harmonic progressions, dissonant harmony, and complex rhythms. Some of the prominent names in bop music were Charlie Parker, Dizzy Gillespie, Miles Davis, and Art Tatum.

*Jazz Since 1950.* Since the end of World War II, jazz has undergone a series of numerous and rapidly changing fads, variously labeled progressive jazz, cool jazz, funky hard bop regression, third-stream music, soul jazz, and rock (rock and roll). In general these styles (1) are less dance oriented, (2) have greater variety of medium within relatively small combos, (3) are more diversified in terms of melody, rhythm, and harmony, (4) tend to borrow techniques and forms from "classical music" (especially characteristic of "third-stream" music), and (5) recently incorporate avant-garde developments in electronic and aleatory procedures (see pages 173 and 181).

Jazz festivals have become popular at Newport, Monterey, and other centers. Jazz has recently infiltrated church music.

*Composers and Musicians.* Many of the prominent figures since mid-century can be identified with more than one trend, and most have repeatedly changed their styles. Among these may be mentioned John Lewis and his Modern Jazz Quartet, Gunther Schuller, John Coltrane, Dave Brubeck (*Dialogue for Jazz Combo and Symphony Orchestra*), Rolf Liebermann (*Concerto for Jazz Band and Symphony Orchestra*), Ornette Coleman, Jimmy Giuffre, Bill Russo, Charlie Mingus, Thelonious Monk, Gil Evans, and a host of others.

**Influences of Jazz.** Many "classical" composers have incorporated jazz elements in their music. Some notable examples are John Alden Carpenter's ballets *Skyscrapers* and *Krazy Kat*, Stravinsky's *Ebony Concerto* (composed for Woody Herman's band) and *Ragtime*, Milhaud's *Creation of the World* (*La Création du Monde*), Honegger's *Concertino*, Copland's *Piano Concerto* (1926), Krenek's jazz opera *Jonny Spielt Auf*, and Morton Gould's *Chorale and Fugue in Jazz*. Most of these compositions were written in the "golden age" of jazz in the 1920s. Since then jazz influences have been less prominent.

**Absolute Music.** Romantic program music has largely been replaced by absolute music, a trend allied with neoclassicism.

**Nationalism.** Nationalism has waned. Composers are more eclectic; they have borrowed from other nationalities and exotic regions. Some examples of "internationalism" are Copland's *El Salon Mexico*, Milhaud's *Saudades do Brazil*, Ibert's *Escales*, and the eclecticism of Alan Hovhaness and Henry Cowell.

**Improvisation.** Not since the Baroque has improvisation played such an important role as in the 20th century. It is confined mainly to three areas: improvisation by concert organists (Marcel Dupré, Jean Langlais, and others), jazz, and most recently *aleatory* music.

**Aleatory Music.** *Aleatory music* (also *chance music*) is one of the most radical trends of the century. It is a concept based on random selection of musical materials by the composer, the performer(s), or both. There are neither laws nor limits imposed on the procedures; the possibilities are infinite. In general the composer selects (often by chance: e.g., throwing dice or digital computer programming) certain basic elements or ideas which may be notated in conventional score or, more often, in some contrived set of symbols. One or more performers then "improvise" on these ideas. Each performance is unique; the creation is preserved only through on-the-scene recording (as it is in "hot" improvised jazz). Aleatory music is currently allied with electronic and computer music. It has even transcended musical boundaries when combined with random poetry reading, improvised audience participation, stage antics, and any number of "irrelevancies" or "happenings."

Stockhausen's *Klavierstücke XI* consists of nineteen fragments for piano which can be played in any order, in any of six tempi and dynamic levels, and with various degrees of staccato or legato. His *Zyklus* for one percussion player is a score in circular form which can be read clockwise, counterclockwise, or upside down. *ST/10, 080262,* and *Stratégie* by Yannis Xenakis (1922–    ) are pieces based on mathematical laws of chance and computer indeterminacy, a technique which he calls *stochastic music.* Other examples of aleatory music are György Ligeti's *Atmospheres;* Morton Feldman's *Projection II* for flute, trumpet, violin, and cello (only registers of "high," "middle," and "low" time values and dynamics are indicated); Larry Austin's *Improvisation for Orchestra and Jazz Soloists;* and John Cage's *Concert,* for piano and orchestra, containing a sixty-three-page piano score with eighty-four different "sound-aggregates" to be played in whole, in part, and in any sequence.

**The Absurd.** Musical parallels to "the theater of the absurd" and to certain aspects of painting and sculpture are represented by such "happenings" as Morton Feldman's use of inaudible frequencies in electronic media; Satie's tongue-in-cheek *Vexations,* an eighty second composition to be played 840 times, discovered by John Cage and performed by ten pianists playing continuous twenty-minute shifts for a total of more than eighteen hours; Cage's own *Imaginary Landscape No. 4,* a four-minute piece for twelve radios; and, perhaps the most famous of all, Cage's *4′ 33″* consisting of four minutes and thirty-three seconds of silence, a "sonata" in three "movements" which are indicated to the audience by the pianist opening and closing the keyboard cover between each movement.

**Electronic and Serial Music.** Two other avant-garde developments may be mentioned here: *electronic music* (discussed in Chapter 26 on media) and *serialism* (discussed in Chapter 27 on techniques).

The distinctive sounds of 20th-century music are due in large part to developments in media, some of which represent the most radical innovations in the entire history of music.

### Conventional Media

The changes in conventional media (e.g., orchestra, chamber music, chorus and opera) have not been as radical as the materials, forms, and techniques they employ.

**Symphonic Music.** The symphony orchestra remains one of the most important media. Symphonic compositions are often scored for smaller orchestras than in the late 19th century. The piano and a few other instruments have been added to the percussion section. Instruments in the woodwind, brass, and string choirs have not changed.

The most prominent traits in modern orchestration are (1) more variety of color combinations, (2) greater frequency of change in timbres, and (3) thinner scoring.

A few works have exploited the possibilities of vocal elements without text: Debussy's *Sirènes* and the last movement of Holst's *The Planets.* Several symphonic works have used a speaking part for narrator: Copland's *Lincoln Portrait,* Thomson's *Testament of Freedom,* Prokofiev's *Peter and the Wolf,* Schoenberg's *Survivor from Warsaw,* and Foss's *A Parable of Death.*

Music for the cinema has not contributed substantially to orchestral literature, but a few succesful works derived from movie sound tracks are Copland's *Our Town,* Thomson's *The Plow that Broke the Plains* and *Louisiana Story,* Prokofiev's *Lieutenant Kijé Suite* and *Alexander Nevsky,* and Vaughan Williams's *Antarctic Symphony.*

**Ballet.** Ballet as a dramatic form independent of opera has enjoyed a popularity unknown since 17th-century French court ballets. The revival began in the late 19th century with Russian ballet and music by Tchaikovsky (*Swan Lake, Sleeping Beauty,* and *The Nutcracker*). Modern ballet, which contributes an important literature to symphonic concerts, began with the creations of Diaghilev and Fokine and the music of Stravinsky: *The Firebird, Petrouchka, The Rite of Spring* (*Le Sacre du Printemps*). Other important ballet music includes Stravinsky's *Soldier's Tale* (*L'Histoire du Soldat*), *Pulcinella, Card Game* (*Jeu de Cartes*), *Les Noces, Apollon Musagète,* and *Agon;* Ravel's *Daphnis et Chloé;* Khatchaturian's *Gayne;* Milhaud's *Bull on the Roof* (*Le Boeuf sur le Toît*); Hindemith's *Nobilissima Visione* from the ballet *St. Francis;* Copland's *Appalachian Spring, Billy the Kid,* and *Rodeo;* Thomson's *Filling Station;* Piston's *Incredible Flutist;* William Schuman's *Judith* and *Undertow;* Bernstein's *Fancy Free;* and Arel's *Flux* and *Music for Dancers* (both electronic music).

**Concert Band.** The concert band (also known as symphonic band and symphonic wind ensemble), as distinct from military, marching, and jazz bands, began to receive attention from serious composers around mid-century. Band concerts which earlier had consisted entirely of marches, popular arrangements, and transcriptions of symphonic music, began to program more sophisticated music originally written for that medium.

Examples of symphonic band music by major composers are Hindemith's Symphony in B Flat, Milhaud's *Suite Française* and *West Point Suite,* Barber's *Commando March,* Bennett's *Suite of Old American Dances,* Hanson's *Chorale and Alleluia,* Vaughan Williams's *Toccata Marziale,* Persichetti's *Divertimento for Band,* Thomson's *A Solemn Music,* Schoenberg's *Theme and Variations for Band,* and Dello Joio's *Fantasy on a Theme by Haydn.*

**Chamber Music.** The revival of interest in chamber music is one manifestation of neoclassicism. Being the medium best suited to clear sonorities and contrapuntal textures, it is compatible with classical objectivity. Although the string quartet remains a favorite ensemble, various combinations of wind instruments have also attracted composers, as they did in the 18th-century divertimento. A combination of instruments currently favored among performing groups and composers is the wind quintet consisting of flute, clarinet, oboe, bassoon, and horn, examples of which are Milhaud's *The Hearth of King René* (*La Cheminée du Roi René*), Ibert's *Trois Pièces Brèves*, Stockhausen's *Zeitmesse*, and Villa-Lobos's *Quintet in the Form of a Choro*.

A return to 17th-century tower-sonata media is suggested by such works as Sander's *Quintet in B Flat* and Dahl's *Music for Brass Instruments* (two trumpets, two trombones, and horn).

Chamber orchestras and string orchestras also reflect the neoclassical trend in such works as Vaughan Williams's *Fantasy on a Theme of Thomas Tallis*, Stravinsky's *Apollon Musagète*, Barber's *Adagio for Strings* (orginally the slow movement of his String Quartet, opus 11), Copland's *Quiet City* for trumpet, English horn, and strings, and Kennan's *Night Soliloquy* for flute solo and strings. Other prominent composers of chamber music are Bartók, Hindemith, Schoenberg, Shostakovich, Piston, Porter, Diamond, Kirchner, and Carter.

**Piano Music.** Although the piano is important in ensemble media, music for piano solo does not hold the prominent place it did in 19th-century music. Some noteworthy examples of modern piano literature are Ravel's *Sonatine* and *Le Tombeau de Couperin*, Shoenberg's *Three Piano Pieces* opus 11 (*Drei Klavierstücke*), Bartók's *Mikrokosmos*, Milhaud's *Saudades do Brazil*, Shostakovich's *Twenty-four Preludes and Fugues*, and Hindemith's three sonatas and *Ludus Tonalis*.

**Choral Music.** Although there is a renewed interest in performance of renaissance and baroque choral music, composition in this medium attracts relatively few composers today. Some important choral works, mostly in the oratorio category with solo voices and orchestra, are Stravinsky's *Symphony of Psalms* and *Threni*, Honegger's *King David* and *Joan of Arc at the Stake* (*Jeanne d'Arc au Bûcher*), Walton's *Belshazzar's Feast*, Orff's *Carmina Burana*, Piston's *Carnival Song* (male chorus and brass choir), Hanson's *Lament for Beowulf*, Dallapiccola's *Job*, Poulenc's *Gloria* and *Mass*, Britten's *Festival Te Deum* and *War Requiem*, and Webern's two cantatas.

**Art Song.** The art song has less appeal than it did among the romantic lieder composers; solo song enjoys a far greater following in the popular and folk song areas. Some important song cycles are Debussy's *Chansons de Bilitis*, Hindemith's *Marienleben*, Carpenter's *Gitanjali*, and Barber's *Hermit Songs*. A new medium is the solo song with chamber ensemble accompaniment, such as Vaughan Williams's *On Wenlock Edge* for tenor, piano, and string quartet; Britten's *Serenade* for tenor, horn, and strings; Toch's *Chinese Flute* for soprano and chamber orchestra; and Barber's *Dover Beach* for baritone and string quartet.

**Opera.** Although the repertory of major opera companies still draws predominantly from the 19th century, an impressive number of operas in 20th-century styles has been produced, the first of which was Debussy's impressionist opera *Pelléas et Mélisande* in 1902.

*Serious Opera.* Notable works in the first half of the century are Britten's *Peter Grimes* and *Billy Budd*, Berg's operas *Wozzeck* and *Lulu*, Menotti's *The Medium* and *The Consul*, Stravinsky's *The Rake's Progress*, Schoenberg's *Moses and Aaron*, Orff's *Die Kluge*, Thomson's *Four Saints in Three Acts*, Moore's *The Devil and Daniel Webster*, Janáček's *Kata Kabanová*, and Shostakovich's *Lady Macbeth of Mtzensk*.

Important serious operas produced since 1950 are Menotti's *The Saint of Bleeker Street, Maria Golovin, Amahl and the Night Visitors* composed for television, and *The Last Savage;* Britten's *Curlew River;* Ginastera's *Don Rodrigo;* Poulenc's *The Dialogues of the Carmelites* and *The Human Voice* (*La Voix Humaine,* a tragic telephone monologue); Moore's *The Ballad of Baby Doe;* Carlisle Floyd's *Susannah* and *Of Mice and Men,* Henze's *Boulevard Solitude* and *The Stag King* (*König Hirsch,* a fairy tale opera) and *The Bassarids;* Barber's *Vanessa* and *Anthony and Cleopatra;* and *The Devils of Loudun* by Krzysztof Penderecki (1933– ).

**Comic Opera.** Some important comic operas are Hindemith's *There and Back* (*Hin und Zurück*); Ravel's *Spanish Hour* (*L'Heure Espagnole*); Shostakovitch's *The Nose;* Stravinsky's *Mavra;* and Menotti's *Amelia Goes to the Ball, The Old Maid and the Thief, The Telephone,* and *Help, Help, the Globolinks,* which contains some prerecorded electronic sounds.

*Operetta.* The vogue of operettas and musical comedies, which began with the Gilbert and Sullivan operettas, continued in the 20th century with works by Victor Herbert (1859–1924), H. L. Reginald de Koven (1859–1920), Rudolf Friml (1879–1972), Jerome Kern (1885–1945), Sigmund Romberg (1887–1951), Irving Berlin (1888–    ), Cole Porter (1893–1964), Vincent Youmans (1898–1946), Richard Rogers (1902–    ), Frederick Loewe (1904–    ), and Leonard Bernstein (1918–    ).

*Folk Opera.* Folk opera (also called "grass-roots opera"), based on regional legends and tunes, has had some success in America with such works as Weill's *Down in the Valley*, Gershwin's *Porgy and Bess*, and Foss's *The Jumping Frog of Calaveras County*.

## New Media

Experimentation in media is as significant a trait in music as it is in art. Not only have composers sought new effects with conventional instruments but they have invented sound generators.

**New Combinations.** Composers employ many new combinations of conventional instruments in chamber and orchestral ensembles. A few examples are Pinkham's *Concerto for Celesta and Harpsichord* (without orchestra); Schoenberg's *Serenade* for baritone voice, clarinet, bass clarinet, mandolin, guitar, violin, viola, and cello; Villa Lobos's *Bachianas Brasilerias No. 1* for eight cellos; Bartók's *Music for Strings, Percussion, and Celesta;* and Chávez's *Toccata for Percussion.*

**Unusual Uses of Conventional Instruments.** The urge to create new kinds of sounds led to exploring possibilities of using conventional instruments in unusual ways. For example, Stravinsky opened his *Rite of Spring* with a bassoon solo in the extremely high register. Bartók produced new string effects by combining pizzicato, sul ponticello, col legno, glissando, and harmonics in his third, fourth, and fifth string quartets. Henry Cowell produced exotic sounds by plucking the strings of a grand piano and by glissandi along the length of the wrapped strings, as in *Banshee*. Hovhaness produced interesting effects by using a plectrum and tympani sticks on piano strings while simultaneously using the keyboard in conventional manner (*Pastorale, Orbit No. 2, Jhala*).

John Cage experimented with piano sounds by attaching to the strings such materials as screws, rubber, glass, wood, and cellophane in his *Sonatas for Prepared Piano*. Penderecki composed *Threnody for the Victims of Hiroshima* for string orchestra, making use of extremely high registers and "bands" of adjacent tones played simultaneously.

**Unconventional Instruments.** Bizarre sound-producing objects have been introduced in amazing profusion. An early example is Strauss's use of a wind machine in *Don Quixote*. Varèse calls for a siren in *Ionization*. Water-buffalo bells and brake drums, among other instruments, are used in Cage's *Double Music*. Harry Partch (1901–    ) has invented a variety of instruments (among them, bamboo marimba, cloud chamber bowls, surrogate kithara, Mazda marimba), and he has composed music for them: *Petals Fell in Petaluma* and *Delusion of the Fury*. Music combined with sculpture was exhibited in Europe and America in the 1960s as "Structures for Sound" with beautifully sculptured objects created by François and Bernard Baschet and music to be played on them composed by Jacques Lasry, Daniel Ouzounoff, and Jacques Chollet.

**Electronic Instruments.** This category includes instruments which depend partly or entirely on electric current for tone production, but it excludes more advanced electronic media developed since 1950. (See Tape Recorder Music and Electronic Music, below.) Electronic amplification has been applied to conventional instruments, especially the guitar. A number of instruments which generate tone electronically were invented during the first half of the century, including the Telharmonium, Theremin, Ondes Martinot, Hammond Organ, Novachord, and Vibraharp. Relatively little significant literature has been composed specifically for these instruments.

**Tape Recorder Music.** Shortly before 1950 the magnetic tape recorder, which had been developed as a means of transmitting music and speech, became a medium for composition, opening radically new vistas in music. Called *musique concrète*, it was first developed by Pierre Schaeffer in Paris, and subsequently in other centers, especially in the United States where it is known as *tape recorder music* or simply *tape music*. Its greatest significance for music generally is that the function of the performer is greatly diminished or else eliminated altogether, for the music is created directly on magnetic tape and is heard through that medium (or commercially transferred to discs). Another important feature of tape music is that it contains a large portion of nontonal sounds, melody and harmony being minimal.

*Technique.* The first step in tape music composing is the recording of live sounds: conventional music, natural or contrived sounds such as traffic noise, bird calls, breaking glass, and dropped objects. These sounds are then manipulated by four basic procedures: (1) changing the speed of the tape, (2) reversing its direction, (3) cutting and splicing the tape, and (4) combinations of these devices. Separately recorded sound tracks may then be combined simultaneously on one track.

*Composers.* Names associated with *musique concrète* are Pierre Schaeffer, Pierre Henri, and Pierre Boulez in France; Karlheinz Stockhausen in Germany; Edgar Varèse, Otto Luening, Mel Powell, and Vladimir Ussachevsky in the United States. Examples of tape music are Ussachevsky's *Piece for Tape Recorder* and *Of Wood and Brass;* and *Suite from King Lear* by Luening and Ussachevsky.

**Electronic Music.** The most recent and radical departures from conventional media are in electronic music. Unlike tape music which takes live sounds from the air, electronic music, in its strict sense, begins with electronically generated sounds. Along with tape music, it has created a totally new field of aesthetics, for it is not only a new media but also a new way of composing, and it requires new attitudes of listening. It involves such a diversity and complexity of esoteric ideas and techniques that only the most rudimentary aspects can be summarized here.

*Kinds of Sound.* Electronic music, like conventional music, recognizes four properties: pitch (vibration frequency), amplitude (dynamics, the property of loudness and softness), duration, and timbre (tone quality).

Five kinds of sound waves can be produced electronically at any level of pitch and dynamics, and for any duration: (1) *sinusoidal wave* (pure tone, no overtones), (2) *square wave* (fundamental and odd-numbered overtones), (4) *composite wave* (certain selected overtones), and (5) *irregular wave* or *white sound* (nontonal sound), the latter being the most prominent and characteristic element in electronic music. All sounds, electronic or otherwise, have an additional property known in electronic music as *envelope,* which is determined by characteristics of attack and decay.

*Synthesizer.* An important instrument on which electronic music is produced is the *synthesizer,* a complex of oscillators, circuits, filters, and magnetic tape recorders The composer selects the kinds of sounds mentioned above, and through the synthesizer submits them simultaneously to intricate modifications, mixing, amplification, envelope variations, and serialization, the end result of which is a series of composite sounds which are recorded directly on multiple-track magnetic tape. The product of the synthesizer may be further modified by the tape-music techniques described above. Hence, the term "electronic music" now includes tape music.

The first synthesizer was produced by RCA in 1955. A later and still more complex machine with keyboard was invented by Robert Moog in 1969 and is known as the Moog Synthesizer. One of the most important centers of electronic music is the Columbia-Princeton Laboratory in New York.

*Computer.* The digital computer has been added to the resources of electronic music. All aspects of sound production can be programmed into the computer, including factors of chance. An early example of computer-composed music was the *Illiac Suite for String Quartet* composed by Lejaren Hiller in 1956.

*Recent Trends.* Trends in electronic music have been moving toward combining conventional media (voices and instruments) with electronic media, and toward simulating conventional timbres in combination with characteristic electronic sounds. Jazz combos have introduced some elements of electronic music.

*Examples. Agony* by Illhan Mimaroglu (1926–　) is totally electronic music. *Rimes* by Henri Pousseur (1929–　) combines conventional instruments with electronic sounds. *Kontakte II* by Stockhausen is entirely electronic, but it simulates some conventional timbres. In his *Synchronisms* Mario Davidovsky (1934–　) uses solo instruments and tape-recorded electronic sounds. Luciano Berio (1925–　) employed nontextual tape-recorded vocal sounds combined with electronic sounds in *Visage.* In *Ensembles for Synthesizer,* Milton Babbitt (1916–　) used the tempered scale and a minimum of white wave sound. Otto Luen-ing's *Gargoyles* was composed for conventional violin solo (un-distorted) and synthesized sound.

Other composers prominent in the electronic field are John Donald Robb (1892–    ), Ussachevsky, Cage, Yannis Xenakis, Krzysztof Penderecki, Gyorgy Ligeti (1923–    ), Joji Yuasa, and Toshi Ichiyanagi (1933–    ), who composed an electronic piece entitled *Tokyo 1969.*

# CHAPTER 27

# Specific Techniques

In addition to general trends outlined in Chapter 25 and developments in medium surveyed in Chapter 26, music of the 20th century has undergone still other changes in compositional techniques. These developments take place in the various elements of music: meter, rhythm, melody, harmony, tonality, texture, and sonority. New concepts of form also come into the picture.

It must be emphasized that not every piece of 20th-century music is a manifestation of radical change in all respects. Any single composition may be "modern" in only one or two respects and not necessarily extreme even in these. The literature ranges from ultra-conservative to avant-garde styles. The largest portion lies somewhere between the extremes.

**Meter and Rhythm.** During the three centuries from 1600 to 1900 (Baroque, Classical, and Romantic eras), little change took place in the time concepts of meter and rhythm. In general, rhythm plays a more prominent role in modern music, and it has greater vitality, complexity, variety, and flexibility. Composers, seeking new rhythmic and metric effects, have overthrown "the tyranny of the bar line" by means of several devices.

*New Time Signatures.* Odd-numbered time signatures, such as $\frac{5}{8}$ and $\frac{7}{8}$, are commonly found in modern scores.

*Asymmetrical Grouping.* New rhythmic effects are produced by asymmetrical grouping of beats or notes within a measure. For example, in $\frac{8}{8}$ meter such patterns as 3-2-2 (rumba) and 3-2-3 produce interesting rhythms. An example is the Scherzo movement of Bartók's Fifth String Quartet which has a time signature

184

indicated as $4+\frac{2}{8}+3$ ( $\frac{9}{8}$ meter), and the Trio section of which is $3+\frac{2}{8}+2+3$ ( $\frac{10}{8}$ meter).

**Nonmetric Music.** Attempting to achieve nonmetric flexibility, as in plainsong, a few composers have omitted the bar line altogether. In conventional media this device is necessarily limited to solo media (Ives's *Concord Sonata*). Most tape and electronic music is nonmetric.

**Polymetric Music.** Polymetric music is that in which two or more meters are used simultaneously. For example, in Ravel's *Piano Trio*, $\frac{3}{4}$ appears against $\frac{4}{2}$. In Stravinsky's *Petrouchka* there are passages of $\frac{5}{8}$ against $\frac{2}{4}$, and $\frac{7}{8}$ against $\frac{3}{4}$.

**Multimetric Music.** This term applies to a fairly common procedure: frequent changes of time signature every measure or so. Examples of multimetric writing are found in Stravinsky's *The Soldier's Tale*, the second movement of Bernstein's *Jeremiah Symphony*, and Webern's Cantata opus 29.

**Displaced Bar Line.** Several devices used with conventional meters produce the effect of shifting or displacing the bar line in the score. Accents may be placed in recurring patterns in conflict with the normal accents of the measure (Example 25a). Similar results can be produced by note grouping (Example 25b), by tying notes across the bar line in prolonged syncopations (Example 25c), or by means of melodic and/or rhythmic ostinato at variance with the meter (Example 25d).

*Example 25. Devices producing displaced bar lines*

An interesting example of the latter device is the "Till" theme in Strauss's *Till Eulenspiegel,* in which a recurrent seven-beat melodic-rhythmic pattern is written in $\frac{6}{8}$ meter.

*Polyrhythmic Music.* In a sense all polyphonic music and even some homophonic music is polyrhythmic because different rhythmic patterns are going on simultaneously. But 20th-century music often exaggerates conflicting rhythms (also called *cross rhythms*). An example of polyrhythmic writing is the movement entitled "Dance" in Copland's *Music for the Theatre* where as many as five different rhythmic patterns, all in $\frac{5}{8}$ meter, oppose one another.

*Combined Effects.* It is apparent that all the above rhythmic and metric devices may be used in various combinations to produce an infinite variety of rhythmic-metric organization.

**Melody.** Departures from earlier melodic concepts involve developments in three areas: (1) melodic style, (2) new scale bases, and (3) the role of melody in the total musical context.

*Style.* Although an appreciable portion of melodic material today is conservative, some distinctly 20th-century characteristics have emerged. More extreme melodic styles feature disjunct progressions (wide leaps from one note to the next), angularity (alternating upward and downward direction) dissonant skips, and fragmentation (small groups of notes separated by rests and widely separated registers). These extremes are illustrated in Example 26.

*Example 26. New melodic style*

*Scale Bases.* Adoption of unconventional scales has contributed to new styles in melody and harmony. Composers have borrowed from the old church modes in neomodal settings. For example, Satie's *Gymnopédie No. 2* is based on the Mixolydian mode. The whole-tone scale (six whole steps to the octave) is used in Debussy's *Violes* and other impressionist compositions. Examples of other new scale systems are Bartók's *Mikrokosmos No. 10* based on a D scale with a key signature of one flat (A flat), and

No. 25 based on a B scale with one sharp (C sharp). Scales using intervals less than a semitone (microtones) have been borrowed from Oriental music. Composers who have written microtonal music are Julian Carrillo, Charles Ives, Hans Barth (*Concerto* for quarter-tone piano and strings), Harry Partch, Penderecki, and others. Discarding tempered scales, electronic music employs microtones and an infinite number of scales with odd intervals.

*The Role of Melody.* Until the 20th century, melody was consistently a dominant element in music. Today its role is variable. It retains its supremacy in contrapuntal textures, but it is subordinate or even nonexistent in some music where rhythm, harmony, and timbre are the prominent elements. Examples of melodic subordination are Honegger's *Pacific 231*, Varèse's *Ionization*, and Chávez's *Toccata for Percussion*. More radical yet is the virtual exclusion of melody in much electronic music, which emphasizes nontonal sounds.

**Harmony.** No element of music has undergone more radical change than harmony. New harmonic concepts involve four approaches: (1) chord construction, (2) chord progression, (3) dissonance, and, in extreme instances, (4) elimination of harmony (electronic music).

*Chord Construction.* For at least three centuries before 1900, chords were built on a tertial basis (superimposed thirds). Chord vocabulary was expanded in the 20th century by further addition of thirds (eleventh and thirteenth chords), quartal harmony (superimposed fourths, such as Scriabin's "mystic chord" containing the tones c-f♯-b♭-e-a-d), and other intervallic bases such as fifths, sevenths, seconds (*tone clusters*), and others. Still further, all intervallic systems were ultimately abandoned in favor of tone combinations of heterogeneous intervals precluding a root basis of construction. Also, mixed chords (or *polychords*) of two or more different roots have been used (for example, superimposing the triad c-e-g and f♯-a♯-c♯, as in the famous "Petrouchka chord").

*Chord Progression.* Conventional root progressions have been largely abandoned in favor of arbitrary progressions, often involving chords with roots foreign to the key, such as E-flat or G-sharp triads in the key of C major. Quite modern harmonic effects can be achieved solely by means of unconventional progressions, even those employing only simple triads. *Parallelism,* an archaism similar to early organum and fauxbourdon, results when the intervals of a tone combination remain consultant as they move in parallel motion. Two or more parallel progressions moving independently at the same time are called *chord streams.*

**Dissonance.** A distinct characteristic of modern harmony is the extent and degree to which dissonance is employed. Dissonant harmony no longer requires resolution to consonance, and a composition may consist only of varying degrees of dissonance.

**Nonharmonic Music.** That electronic music which is confined to nontonal sounds has eliminated the harmonic element altogether, for "white wave" sounds can create neither harmony nor melody.

**Tonality.** Tonality (key feeling, or the gravitation around the tonic) began to show signs of weakening during the 19th century. Chromatic harmony and prolonged modulations increasingly obscured the tonal center. The 20th century has departed still further from conventional tonal concepts, ultimately eliminating tonal centers.

**Harmonic Aspects.** Harmonic innovations which contributed to tonal obscurity were neomodality, microtonality, new scale bases, and more intense and prolonged use of dissonance.

**Polytonality.** The simultaneous use of two or more keys, called *polytonality,* was a 20th-century innovation. Since its heyday in the 1920s, polytonality has been absorbed in other techniques. Notable proponents of polytonality were Milhaud and Honegger. Examples are Prokofiev's *Sarcasms* opus 17, no. 3 (B-flat minor in the left hand, F-sharp minor in the right hand), and the third of Milhaud's *Cinq Symphonies,* which opens with the keys of E major (clarinet), D major (bassoon), and E-flat major (strings).

**Atonality.** The ultimate development is *atonality,* the absence of any key center or key feeling. Although 20th-century music ranges from completely tonal to completely atonal, the larger portion today falls closer to the latter.

**Texture.** Although homophonic textures are not uncommon in 20th-century music, contrapuntal textures dominate. An attribute of neoclassicism is the renewed interest in contrapuntal forms of the Baroque such as fugue, canon, and passacaglia.

**Sonority.** Another attribute of neoclassicism is the predominance of clear, thin, and transparent sonorities, resembling those of

18th-century classicism as opposed to the heavy sonorities of the 19th century. An extremely thin sonority called *pointillism* is produced by a combination of few tones sounding simultaneously, disjunct and fragmentary lines, widely spaced registers, and frequently changed timbres. An example of pointillism is Webern's *Concerto for Nine Instruments*.

**Serialism.** Music constructed on the basis of a recurrent series of tones, rhythms, dynamics, or timbres (or a combination of these) is called serial music. Serialism, which began in the 1920s with Schoenberg's twelve-tone system, is related both to atonality and to new concepts of formal structure in music.

**Twelve-Tone Music.** The adjectives *twelve-tone, tone-row,* and *dodecaphonic* refer to music based on a series of twelve different pitches called a *tone row*, or simply *row*. A tone row contains all twelve tones of the octave arranged in such an order that any implication of tonic or key center is avoided. Melody, harmony, and themes are derived from the tone row, which replaces scales as the basis of composition. The original row (O) of a composi-

*Example 27. Manipulations of the tone row*

tion is subject to the following modifications: transposition (T), octave transposition (OT) of any tones in the row, retrogradation of the row as a whole (R) or by consecutive groups of twos, threes, fours, or sixes, inversion (I), and combinations of these such as retrograde inversion (RI). The row and its basic manipulations are illustrated in Example 27.

*Multiple Serialism.* Since Webern, who added rhythmic serialization to the tone-row principle, composers have expanded the number of musical elements serialized to include recurrent patterns of dynamics, timbre, and density (sonorities). In total serialization all elements are serialized. The most complex serial music is that in which two or more series are not synchronized within a given time span. Example 28 illustrates such serial

*Example 28. Multiple serialization*

organization. Series 1 is a tone row; series 2 is a recurrent rhythmic pattern of four beats (in $\frac{3}{4}$ meter); series 3 is a simple pattern of dynamic gradations lasting seven beats; and series 4 is a cycle of three timbres in a series approximately four bars long. Longer patterns, manipulations of the row, and the addition of harmony and density series could be employed in a more complex total serialism. Such serial organization has been exploited especially in electronic and computer music.

*Composers.* Since 1950 a large number of composers have employed various serial techniques. Among these are Messiaen and Boulez in France; Pousseur in Belgium; Stockhausen and Fortner in Germany; Dallapiccola, Berio, Nono, and Maderna in Italy; and Riegger, Krenek, Weiss, Kerr, Wolpe, and Babbitt in the United States.

*Form.* Although contrapuntal forms have a significant place in neoclassicism, and classical sectional structures (e.g., sonata form, variations, rondos) have by no means been abandoned, still, 20th-century composers have generally avoided conventional forms or else greatly modified them. In addition to serialism, several traits of modern form may be mentioned. Defined as the avoidance of conventional cadences and other indications of sectional division, *nonperiodicity* is a significant characteristic of form. Related to nonperiodic structure is the concept of perpetual variation in which exact sectional repetition is studiously avoided and the musical materials undergo continual modification. Asymmetrical structures also are typical. These characteristics, along with atonality and multiple serialism, result in the negation of perceptible structural organization in much contemporary music. This is especially true of electronic and aleatory music where the listener is unable to perceive any structural basis or systematic organization of the musical materials.

# CHAPTER 28

# Summary of Principal Twentieth-Century Composers

This chapter lists, in alphabetical order, twenty countries prominent in 20th-century music. Composers in each country who attained special eminence before 1950 are mentioned first, and their significance briefly noted. Other important composers are listed chronologically by year of birth.

**Argentina.** An abundance of folksong material, mostly of Gaucho origin, provides a rich source of native material used by Argentine composers.

*Alberto Ginastera (1916– ).* Ginastera has blended native color with moderately dissonant but tonal harmonies. Among his many successful works are *Panambi, Concierto Argentino,* and *Pampeana No. 3.*

*Other Composers:* Alberto Williams (1862–1952), Juan Castro (1895–1968), Juan Carlos Paz (1897– ), Carlos Suffern (1905– ), Roberto Morillo (1911– ), Carlos Guastavino (1914– ).

**Austria.** Having produced famous composers in the Renaissance and Baroque, having dominated the Viennese classical period (Haydn and Mozart), and having continued to be a power in 19th-century music, Austria maintains its position with some celebrated 20th-century musicians.

*Arnold Schoenberg (1874–1951).* One of the most influential men of the century, Schoenberg began with post-Wagnerian music (*Transfigured Night*), moved toward atonality and into expressionism in the second decade, and established the twelve-tone system in the early 1920s. He initiated a vocal style called *Sprechstimme* or *Sprechgesang* (half-spoken, half-sung text) which he employed first in *Pierrot Lunaire* and later in *Survivor from Warsaw* for narrator, chorus, and orchestra.

*Alban Berg (1885–1935).* A pupil of Schoenberg, Berg employed the tone-row system freely, and his music is generally more romantic and more tonal than Schoenberg's. His most famous works are the two operas *Wozzeck* and *Lulu, Lyric Suite* for string quartet, and the *Violin Concerto.*

*Anton Webern (1883–1945).* Also a pupil of Schoenberg, Webern composed in a more stringent style, employed dissonant counterpoint, disjunct melodic lines, severe economy of means, and pointillistic texture. He was not a prolific composer, but his music has had a profound influence on composers since 1950.

*Ernst Krenek (1900– ).* An illustrious and versatile composer, Krenek has been active in the United States since 1937 as teacher, scholar, and composer of atonal serial music. He won early fame with a jazz opera, *Jonny Spielt Auf* in 1927. A more recent work is *Pentagram* for woodwind quintet.

*Other Composers:* Franz Schreker (1878–1934), Josef Hauer (1883–1959), Ernst Toch (1887–1964, in the United States from 1933), Gottfried von Einem (1918– ).

**Belgium.** Since its heyday in the Renaissance, Belgian music has not attained much musical eminence. Among prominent modern composers are Paul Gilson (1865–1942), Joseph Jongen (1873–1953), Paul de Maleingreau (1887–1956), Jean Absil (1893– ), Marcel Poot (1901– ), and Henri Pousseur, who is an important avant-garde composer.

**Brazil.** Brazilian music is a mixture of African, Portuguese, and native Indian cultures, all of which have been stylistic sources.

*Heitor Villa-Lobos (1887–1959).* The most illustrious among Brazilian composers, Villa-Lobos was a conservative nationalist, drawing from the various ethnic sources of his country. Among his highly individualistic works are fourteen compositions called *Choros* for various media, and nine compositions entitled *Bachianas Brasileiras,* also for diverse media.

*Other Composers:* Francisco Mignone (1897– ), Camargo Guarnieri (1907– ), Guerra Peixe (1914– ), Claudio Santoro

(1919–   ), Gilberto Mendes (1922–   ), Osvaldo Lacerda (1927–   ), Damiano Cozzella (1929–   ), Roger Duprat (1932–   ), and Marlos Nobre (1939–   ).

**Canada.** The leading names among Canadian composers are Healey Willan (1880–1968), Colin McPhee (1901–1964), Barbara Pentland (1912–   ), John Weinzweig (1913–   ), Alexander Brott (1915–   ), Jean Vallerand (1915–   ), Jean Papineau-Couture (1916–   ), Godfrey Ridout (1918–   ), Harry Sommers (1925–   ), and Pierre Mercure (1927–   ).

**Czechoslovakia.** Czech music has remained predominantly conservative, romantic, and strongly nationalistic in the 20th century.

*Leoš Janáček (1854–1923).* Janáček's music has received widespread acclaim since his death. Though strongly nationalist, his style evolved toward more modern techniques. His principal works are the opera *Jenufa* and the *Glagolitic Mass.*

*Bohuslav Martinů (1890–1959).* Influenced by impressionism and somewhat by Stravinsky, Martinů made use of native folk idiom in his operas (*Comedy on a Bridge*), symphonies, ballets, and chamber works.

*Other Composers:* Josef Suk (1874–1935), Alois Hába (1893–   ), who was a microtonalist, Jaromir Weinberger (1896–1967) who is famous for the opera *Schwanda the Bagpiper,* Miloslav Kabeláč (1908–   ), Eugen Suchon (1908–   ), Karel Reiner (1910–   ), Václav Kaslik (1917–   ).

**England.** England's high position in music, which declined after the Renaissance, has been restored in the 20th century.

*Ralph Vaughan Williams (1872–1958).* Generally considered the most eminent English composer in the first half of the century, Vaughan Williams composed moderately conservative, romantic, and consistently tonal music. English folk-song idioms are evident in much of his music. He excelled in symphonic and choral media. One of his most popular compositions is the *Fantasy on a Theme of Thomas Tallis* for string orchestra.

*William Walton (1902–   ).* Walton stands high on the list of illustrious English composers born in the first decade of the century. Generally conservative, he has assimilated a number of modern techniques in his highly personal style. Among his many successful works are *Façade* for chamber orchestra with recited poems by Edith Sitwell, the oratorio *Belshazzar's Feast,* the opera *Troilus and Cressida,* and music for the films *Henry V* and *Romeo and Juliet.*

**Benjamin Britten (1913–1976).** Britten is widely recognized as a major composer who has produced a number of excellent large-scale works, especially the operas *Billy Budd, Peter Grimes, The Rape of Lucretia, Noye's Fludde,* and others. His *Young Person's Guide to the Orchestra* is a clever orchestral variations and fugue on a theme by Purcell.

**Other Composers:** Frederick Delius (1862–1934), Gustav Holst (1874–1934), Arnold Bax (1883–1953), Arthur Bliss (1891–   ), Alan Bush (1900–   ), Edmund Rubbra (1901–   ), Michael Tippett (1905–   ), Alan Rawsthorne (1905–71), Elisabeth Lutyens (1906–   ), Humphrey Searle (1915–   ), Richard Arnell (1917–   ), Peter Racine Fricker (1920–   ), Malcolm Arnold (1921–   ), Anthony Milner (1925–   ), Malcolm Williamson (1931–   ), Peter Maxwell Davies (1934–   ), Richard Bennett (1936–   ).

**France.** France was the undisputed leader in the Middle Ages, sustained eminence in the Renaissance and Baroque, and in the 20th century again has been in the front ranks of musical nations. French composers were the first to turn from the dominance of German romanticism to new modes of musical thought, and they were pioneers in *musique concrète.*

**Claude Debussy (1862–1918).** Debussy, the foremost impressionist composer, represents the threshold of modernism much in the same way that Beethoven represents the transition from classical to romantic music. His innovations (see "Impressionism," page 168), revolutionary in their day, opened the door to 20th-century experimentation. Debussy's principal areas of composition were piano and orchestra, in which he introduced new harmonies and sonorities. His best-known orchestral works are the symphonic poem *Prelude to the Afternoon of a Faun (Prélude à l'Après-midi d'un Faune),* and the orchestral suites *The Sea (La Mer)* and *Nocturnes.* His *Préludes* with descriptive titles are important contributions to piano literature.

**Maurice Ravel (1875–1937).** Ravel's style transcends impressionism, to which he added neoclassical clarity, colorful orchestration, and a considerable use of Spanish elements. His best-known works are the piano pieces *Tombeau de Couperin* and *Sonatine,* and the orchestral works *Mother Goose Suite* (*Ma Mère l'Oye,* originally for piano duet), *Rhapsodie Espagnole,· Boléro, La Valse,* and the ballet *Daphnis et Chloé.*

**Les Six.** In the 1920s a group of six composers initiated an anti-impressionist movement of a neoclassical nature. "The Six" were Darius Milhaud, Arthur Honegger (1892–1955), Francis Poulenc (1899–1963), Germaine Tailleferre (1892–    ), Georges Auric (1899–    ), and Louis Durey (1888–    ). The first three became eminent composers. Erik Satie (1866–1925), composer, and Jean Cocteau, author, critic, and dramatist, were associated with the group.

**Darius Milhaud** (*1892–1974*). Milhaud is the most eminent, versatile, and prolific composer among *Les Six.* He has composed music in all media and virtually all 20th-century styles. He was a proponent of polytonality in the 1920s. Though consistently Gallic in spirit, he is an eclectic cosmopolite who absorbed idioms from Brazil, jazz, and other indigenous elements, including those of his native Provence.

Composers whose creative lives belong mostly to the 20th century but who stylistically belong more to the 19th century are Gustave Charpentier, Joseph Guy Ropartz (1864–1955), Paul Dukas (1865–1935), Charles Koechlin (1867–1950), Henri Rabaud (1873–1949), Jean Roger-Ducasse (1873–1954), and Henri Duparc. Special mention should be made of Eric Satie, Albert Roussel (1869–1937), Florent Schmitt (1870–1958), Maurice Duruflé (1902–    ), André Jolivet (1905–74), Olivier Messiaen (1908–    ), Jean Françaix (1912–    ), and Pierre Boulez (1925–    ).

**Germany.** The importance of German-speaking nations, including Austria, has been noted from the time of the Minnesingers to the present. During the two global wars, German music was in partial eclipse, but has since 1950 come again into prominence.

**Paul Hindemith** (*1895–1963*). Following the domination of Richard Strauss in the early decades, Hindemith stands as the most eminent representative of German music in the first half of the century. His name has been mentioned in connection with the trends of neoclassicism and Gebrauchsmusik. Among his masterpieces are the Symphony *Mathis der Maler,* the opera *Cardillac,* and *Ludus Tonalis* for piano.

*Other Composers:* Carl Orff (1895–     ), Werner Egk (1901–    ), Boris Blacher (1903–75), Karl Hartman (1905–63), Giselher Klebe (1925–    ), and Wolfgang Fortner (1907–    ). Special mention should be made of two composers who have become prominent since 1950: Hans Werner Henze (1926–    ) mostly in the field of opera, and Karl Heinz Stockhausen (1928–    ) in the areas of serial, electronic, and aleatory music.

**Greece.** Since its great contributions to musical antiquity, Greece has played no important role in the history of music. Some names in modern Greek music are George Lamblet (1875–1945), Manolis Kalomiris (1883–1962), Mario Varvoglis (1885–1967), Nikos Skalkottas (1904–49), Manos Hadzidakis (1925–    ), and Yannis Xenakis, who is an avant-garde composer in serial, electronic, and aleatory music.

**Holland.** Illustrious Dutch names such as Ockeghem and Obrecht in the 15th century and Sweelinck in the early Baroque are notable in earlier history. Important names in the 20th century are Hendrik Andriessen (1892–    ), Willem Pijper (1894–1947), and Henk Badings (1907–    ).

**Hungary.** Hungary, never prominent in music history, has produced some distinguished composers in the 20th century.

*Béla Bartók (1881–1945).* A top-rank pianist, collector of Balkan folk music, teacher, and composer, Bartók remains one of the giants of modern music. He was never a "systems" composer conforming to trends (impressionist, neoclassicist) or techniques (serialism, polytonality). He was always imbued with Hungarian idiom and a strong spirit of individualism. His music taken as a whole represents most of the modern techniques in melody, harmony, rhythm, tonality, and textures, but he never adopted dodecaphonic technique. Among his masterpieces are *Mikrokosmos* (153 graded pieces for piano), six *String Quartets*, and the justly famous *Music for Strings, Percussion, and Celesta.*

*Zoltán Kodály (1882–1967).* Kodály followed in Bartók's footsteps as a modern Hungarian nationalist, though somewhat more conservative. His principal works are the opera *Háry János, Psalmus Hungaricus* for tenor solo, chorus, children's voices, and orchestra, and *Dances of Galanta.*

*Other Composers:* Ernst von Dohnányi (1877–1960), Leo Weiner (1885–1960), Tibor Serly (1900–    ), Paul Kadosa

(1903–    ), and György Ligeti (1923–    ) a renowned avant-garde composer (*Artikulation* for electronic sounds).

**Italy.** Italy shared leadership with France in the Ars Nova, began and dominated the Renaissance, initiated the nuove musiche revolution at the beginning of the 17th century, led the world in opera, but became a musically conservative nation in the first decades of the 20th century. Toward mid-century, Italian composers once again came into the current of contemporary developments.

*Ferruccio Busoni* (*1866–1924*). Busoni was the foremost spokesman of modern Italian music. Influential as composer, pianist, editor, critic, and teacher, he pointed the way to new musical thought in Italy.

*Ottorino Respighi* (*1879–1936*). Respighi was Italy's first important instrumental composer in the 20th century, although conservative in terms of then current practices. His best-known works are the two symphonic poems (each in four continuous movements) *The Pines of Rome* and *The Fountains of Rome,* and the *Concerto Gregoriano.*

*Francesco Malipiero* (*1882–1973*). Malipiero is an eminent musicologist who made scholarly studies and editions of Italian baroque composers (Monteverdi, Vivaldi, and others). These studies influenced the neoclassicism of his own compositions, which include operas, symphonies, large choral works (*La Cena*), and chamber music.

*Alfredo Casella* (*1883–1947*). Another neoclassicist was Casella, who returned to baroque forms and counterpoint but with moderately dissonant harmonies. Notable works are *Concerto Romano* and *Scarlattiana* for piano and orchestra.

*Other Composers:* Leone Sinigaglia (1868–1944), Ermanno Wolf-Ferrari (1876–1948), Ildebrando Pizzetti (1880–1968), Vittorio Rieti (1898–    ), Goffredo Petrassi (1904–    ). Gian Carlo Menotti (1911–    ) has studied, resided, and produced most of his operas in the United States. Special mention should be made of currently important avant-garde composers in serial and electronic composition: Luigi Dallapiccola (1904–    ), Bruno Maderna (1920–    ), Luigi Nono (1924–    ), and Luciano Berio.

**Japan.** Since World War II, Japan has shown an affinity for Western music. Japan has produced some important performing artists, conductors, and composers. Among the latter are Yuji Takahashi (1938–  , *Orphika* for orchestra); Toru Takemitsu (1930–  , *Asterism* for piano and orchestra); Hikary Hiyashi (1931–  ); Toshi Ichiyangi (1933–  , *Tokyo 1969* for mixed media including computer generated sound, rock band, and a fourteen-channel distribution system with sequencer); Joji Yuasa (*Icon* for five-channel tape); and Toshiro Mayuzumi (1929–  ), whose *Aoi-No-Ue* is electronic music.

**Mexico.** Mexican music, like that of other Latin American countries, manifests a strong nationalist strain which blends indigenous elements with Spanish and conservatively modern styles.

*Carlos Chávez* (*1899–*    ). Chávez is Mexico's foremost musician, an educator, organizer, conductor, and composer. He is a neoclassical nationalist who has composed in a variety of media. His best known works are *Sinfonia India, Sinfonia de Antigona,* and *Xochipilli Macuilxochitl* for native instruments.

*Silvestre Revueltas* (*1899–1940*). Mexican folklore and idiom are essential ingredients in Revueltas's music. His most famous works are *Cuauhnahuac* and *Sensemaya,* both for orchestra.

*Other Composers:* Julian Carrillo (1875–1965), famous for his microtonal music, Manuel Ponce (1882–1948), Daniel Ayala (1908–  ), Miguel Jimenez (1910–56), Blas Galindo (1910–  ), Salvador Contreras (1912–  ), Pablo Moncayo (1912–58).

**Poland.** Except for a few isolated names (Chopin, Paderewski, Szymanowski), Poland has been largely independent of European trends in music. Some important names in 20th-century music are Karol Szymanowski (1882–1937), Karol Rathaus (1895–1954), Alexander Tansman (1897–  ), Witold Lutoslawski (1913–  ), and Krzysztof Penderecki, an avant-garde composer who has gained considerable recognition outside Poland.

**Russia.** Russia came significantly into the European musical scene in the 19th century. In the 20th century it has been mostly outside the main stream of avant-garde developments because the Soviet government has frowned on revolutionary modernisms which would remove music from the sphere of the proletariat. Nevertheless, Russia has produced great musicians, performing artists, conductors, and composers.

*Igor Stravinsky* (*1882–1971*). Despite its general conservatism, it was Russia which produced the most eminent and often radical composer of the 20th century. Stravinsky, who emigrated to Paris in 1910 and to the United States in 1939, can justly be called an international composer. He has probably had a more profound impact on 20th-century music than any other composer except Schoenberg. A versatile composer in all media, it was in ballet music that his fame was first established. Although his style has repeatedly changed, there are certain traits which have remained prominent in his music: strong and often complex rhythm, use of ostinato, brilliant orchestration, and pungent harmonies. A number of consecutive stylistic trends can be noted: (1) the Russian period, in which he was strongly influenced by Rimsky-Korsakov (*Firebird* and *Fireworks*), (2) the so-called dynamistic period of the then radical *Rite of Spring* (*Le Sacre du Printemps*) and *Petrouchka*, (3) the neoclassical period of the *Octet for Winds*, *The Soldier's Tale* (*L'Histoire du Soldat*), *Pulcinella*, and *Apollon Musagète*, (4) the jazz-influenced music of *Ragtime*, *Ebony Concerto*, *Dumbarton Oaks*, and most recently (5) the use of serial technique in such works as *Agon* and *Threni*. Among his many recognized masterpieces should also be mentioned the *Symphony of Psalms* for chorus and orchestra.

*Sergei Prokofiev* (*1891–1953*). Like Stravinsky, Prokofiev emigrated and lived in the United States and Paris between 1918 and 1934, but he returned to Russia to become one of its most distinguished composers. Among his most popular compositions are *Lieutenant Kijé*, *Peter and the Wolf* (a fairy tale for narrator and orchestra), and the opera *The Love for Three Oranges*.

*Dmitri Shostakovich* (*1906–1975*). Shostakovich's music has had varied reception in Russia, ranging from enthusiastic acclaim to denouncement. On the whole, he has been able to infuse his music with moderately progressive styles while retaining popular appeal. Among his best known works abroad are the opera *Lady Macbeth of Mzensk*, the *Fifth* and *Seventh* ("*Leningrad*") *Symphonies*, the ballet *The Golden Age*, the Piano Quintet, and the twenty-four *Preludes* for piano.

*Other Composers:* Mikhail Ippolitov-Ivanov (1859–1935), Alexander Gretchaninov, Alexander Glazunov, Alexander Scriabin, Sergei Vasilenko (1872–1956), Nicholas Tcherepnin (1873–1945), Reinhold Glière, Nicolai Miaskovsky (1881–1950), Mikhail

Gnessin (1883–1957), Aram Khatchaturian (1903–    ), Dmitri Kabalevsky (1904–    ). More recent names on the Russian scene, some of which are associated with electronic and aleatory music, are Tikhon Khrennikov (1913–    ), Edison Denisov (1929–    ), Sergey Slonimsky (1932–    ), Andrey Volkonsky (1933–    ), Leonid Grabovsky (1935–    ), and Valentin Silvestrov (1937–    ).

**Spain.** Spain's greatest period in music history was the Renaissance, especially in sacred polyphony and vihuela composition. The musicologist Felipe Pedrell (1841–1922) awakened interest in Spanish music history and produced scholarly studies and editions of early masters (Victoria, Morales, Milan, and others). Spanish music of the 20th century is generally conservative and nationalist in style.

*Manuel de Falla (1876–1946).* The most outstanding Spanish composer in the first half of the century was Manuel de Falla. His principal works are the opera *Life Is Short (La Vida Breve)*, the ballets *Three-Cornered Hat (El Sombrero de Tres Picos)*, and *Bewitched by Love (El Amor Brujo)*, and *Nights in the Gardens of Spain (Noches en los Jardines de España)* for piano and orchestra.

*Carlos Surinach (1915–    ).* Surinach, who emigrated to the United States in 1951, is probably the composer best known outside Spain since mid-century. His music combines a nationalist approach with progressive but not extreme techniques. His best known works are the dance-oriented *Sinfonietta Flamenca, Ritmo Jondo, Feria Mágica,* and *Fandango.*

*Other Composers:* Joaquín Turina (1882–1949), Oscar Esplá (1886–    ), Rodolfo Halffter (1900–    ), Julian Bautista (1901–61), and Ernesto Halffter (1905–    ).

**Switzerland.** In the early Middle Ages the Swiss Abbey of St. Gall was an important center of plainsong, tropes, and sequences (Tuotillo, Balbulus). Since then a long line of eminent Swiss composers has firmly established it as an important musical country. Mention should be made of Emile Jaques-Dalcroze (1865–1950) who invented the widely used educational rhythmic-solfège system bearing his name.

*Frank Martin (1890–1974).* Martin is the most important Swiss composer of the century (excluding expatriots such as Honegger, Block, and others). He employs a modified twelve-tone technique in a personalized manner. His *Petite Symphonie Concertante* for harp, harpsichord, piano, and strings is his best known work.

**Rolf Liebermann** (*1910–* ). Liebermann's style is based mainly on dodecaphonic technique combined with classic and romantic elements and a strong rhythmic sense. His most famous work is the *Concerto for Jazz Band and Symphony Orchestra.*

**Other Composers:** Wladimir Vogel (1896– ), a Russian-born serial composer living in Switzerland, Albert Moeschinger (1897– ), Willy Burkhard (1900–55), Conrad Beck (1901– ), Heinrich Sutermeister (1911– ), Jacques Wildberger (1922– ), and Rudolf Kelterborn (1931– ).

**The United States.** The United States has become one of the leading musical nations, having achieved excellence in music education, performance, publication, acoustical technology, musicology, and composition. A relatively young country of heterogeneous cultures, it lacks a traditional and unified nationalism. In the 19th century and early decades of the 20th century, American music was wholly indebted to European sources in the training of its musicians and composers. From this predominantly European heritage American composers emerged as individualists with strongly eclectic tastes. Along with conservative trends, there are significant avant-garde developments in the United States today.

*Traditionalists.* Composers who belong mainly to romantic European tradition are Dudley Buck (1839–1909), John Knowles Paine (1839–1906), Arthur Foote (1853–1937), George Chadwick (1854–1931), Edgar Stillman Kelley (1857–1944), Charles Loeffler, Edward MacDowell, Horatio Parker (1863–1919), Amy (Mrs. Henry) Beach (1867–1944), Henry Gilbert (1868–1928), Frederick Converse (1871–1940), Henry Hadley (1871–1937), Arthur Farwell (1872–1952), Edward Burlingame Hill (1872–1960), Daniel Gregory Mason (1873–1953), and David Stanley Smith (1877–1949).

*Later Generations.* Since about 1920 well over a hundred American composers attained widespread recognition, a fact that precludes even a thumbnail sketch of their music in this outline. Although different authorities would compile quite different lists, a random selection of a dozen composers who for diverse reasons have achieved special eminence might include the names of Riegger, Moore, Piston, Cowell, Harris, Gershwin, Copland,

Barber, Menotti, Dello Joio, Bernstein, and Carter (excluding the major avant-garde composers on the current scene).

Chronologically listed by date of birth, the principal composers are Charles Ives (1874–1954), John Alden Carpenter (1876–1951), Carl Ruggles (1876–   ), Ernest Bloch (1880–1959), Edgar Varèse (1883–1965), Charles T. Griffes (1884–1920), Louis Gruenberg (1884–1964), Wallingford Riegger (1885–1961), Deems Taylor (1885–1966), John Becker (1886–1961), Richard Donovan (1891–1970), Adolph Weiss (1891–1971), Ferde Grofé (1892–1972), Douglas Moore (1893–1969), Paul Pisk (1893–   ), Bernard Rogers (1893–1968), Walter Piston (1894–1976), William Grant Still (1895–   ), Howard Hanson (1896–   ), Roger Sessions (1896–   ), Virgil Thomson (1896–   ), Henry Cowell (1897–1965), Harrison Kerr (1897–   ), Quincy Porter (1897–1966), Ernst Bacon (1898–   ), George Gershwin (1898–1937), Roy Harris (1898–   ), Randall Thompson (1899–   ), George Antheil (1900–59), Aaron Copland (1900–   ), Otto Luening (1900–   ), Harry Partch (1901–74), Stefan Wolpe (1902–72), Marc Blitzstein (1905–64), Paul Creston (1906–   ), Ross Lee Finney (1906–   ), Normand Lockwood (1906–   ), Elliott Carter (1908–   ), Halsey Stevens (1908–   ), Ray Green (1909–   ), Herbert Haufrecht (1909–   ), Paul Nordoff (1909–   ), Elie Siegmeister ·(1909–   ), Howard Swanson (1909–   ), Samuel Barber (1910–   ), Paul Bowles (1910–   ), Bernhard Heiden (1910–   ), William Schuman (1910–   ), Alan Hovhaness (1911–   ), Robert McBride (1911–   ), Gian Carlo Menotti (1911–   ), Ingolf Dahl (1912–70), Arthur Berger (1912–   ), John Cage (1912–   ), Don Gillis (1912–   ), Australia-born Peggy Glanville-Hicks (1912–   , in the United States since 1939), Hugo Weisgall (1912–   ), Norman Dello Joio (1913–   ), Morton Gould (1913–   ), Gardner Read (1913–   ), Everett Helm (1913–   ), Kurt List (1913–70), Kent Kennan (1913–   ), Norman Cazden (1914–   ), Irving Fine (1914–62), Roger Goeb (1914–   ), Gail Kubik (1914–   ), Charles Mills (1914–   ), David Diamond (1915–   ), Homer Keller (1915–   ), Robert Palmer (1915–   ), George Perle (1915–   ), Vincent Persichetti (1915–   ), Milton Babbitt (1916–   ), Ellis Kohs (1916–   ), Ben Weber (1916–   ), Lou Harrison (1917–   ),

Ulysses Kay (1917– ), Robert Ward (1917– ), Leonard Bernstein (1918– ), Frank Wigglesworth (1918– ), Jacob Avshalomov (1919– ), Leon Kirchner (1919– ), Harold Shapero (1920– ), William Bergsma (1921– ), Egyptian-born Halim El Dabh (1921– ), Andrew Imbrie (1921– ), Lukas Foss (1922– ), Chou Wen-Chung (1923– ), Peter Mennin (1923– ), Daniel Pinkham (1923– ), Lester Trimble (1923– ), Ezra Laderman (1924– ), Robert Starer (1924– ), Gunther Schuller (1925– ), Seymour Shifrin (1926– ), and Russell Smith (1927– ).

# Selected Bibliography

This bibliography is designed as a guide to English-language sources of information related to music history. It excludes lists of books in the following categories: biography, instruments, nationalities, and special categories of music literature (e.g., symphony, concerto, chamber music, opera, oratorio, church music). Such information can be obtained from the general and special music histories and the reference works listed here.

The library catalogue is, of course, a primary reference source of locally available materials (books, scores, and recordings). It should be consulted for important subject headings, name entries (authors and composers), and titles.

An important classified bibliography of music bibliographies is Vincent Duckles's *Music Reference and Research Materials*, the Free Press, 2nd ed., 1967.

## Music Dictionaries and Cyclopedias

In addition to essential information about subjects and/or people, the following reference works provide bibliography of books and periodical literature.

Apel, Willi. *Harvard Dictionary of Music*. Harvard University Press, 2nd ed., 1969. A comprehensive dictionary of terms; significant historical information about musical subjects.

Blom, Eric. *Grove's Dictionary of Music and Musicians*, 9 vols., St. Martin's Press, 5th ed., 1954; supplementary vol., 1961. The most comprehensive music cyclopedia in the English language.

Scholes, Percy. *The Oxford Companion to Music*. Edited by John Ward. Oxford University Press, 10th ed., 1970. Extensive cross references and plates.

Slonimsky, Nicholas. *Baker's Biographical Dictionary of Musicians.* G. Schirmer, 5th ed., 1958, with 1971 supplement. A comprehensive and accurate one-volume dictionary of names.

Westrup, Jack, and F. L. Harrison. *The New College Encyclopedia of Music.* Norton, 1960. A concise dictionary of terms and names; music examples, no pictorial material; limited bibliography.

### General Histories of Music

Grout, Donald J. *A History of Western Music.* Norton, 1973.

Lang, Paul Henry. *Music in Western Civilization.* Norton, 1941. Especially valuable for background in political, economic, social, and cultural history.

*The New Oxford History of Music.* Oxford University Press, 1954– . Planned as a ten-volume set written by various authors; three vols. issued to date.

*The Oxford History of Music.* 2nd ed. 8 vols. Oxford University Press, 1929–38.

Sachs, Curt. *Our Musical Heritage.* 2nd ed. Prentice-Hall, 1955.

Ulrich, Homer, and Paul Pisk. *A History of Music and Musical Styles.* Harcourt, Brace & World, 1963.

### Special Historical Periods

Antiquity: Curt Sachs. *The Rise of Music in the Ancient World, East and West.* Norton, 1943.

The Middle Ages: Gustave Reese. *Music in the Middle Ages.* Norton, 1940.

The Renaissance: Gustave Reese. *Music in the Renaissance.* Norton, 1959.

The Baroque: Manfred Bukofzer. *Music in the Baroque Era.* Norton, 1947.

The Classical Era:
> Heger, Theodore. *Music of the Classic Period.* Brown, 1969.
> Pauly, Reinhard. *Music in the Classic Period.* Prentice-Hall, 1965.

The Romantic Era: Alfred Einstein. *Music in the Romantic Era.* Norton, 1947.

The Twentieth Century:

Austin, William. *Music in the 20th Century*. Norton, 1966.

Deri, Otto. *Exploring Twentieth-Century Music*. Holt, Rine-hart & Winston, 1968.

Hansen, Peter. *Twentieth Century Music*. 2nd ed. Allyn & Bacon, 1967.

Machlis, Joseph. *Introduction to Contemporary Music*. Norton, 1961.

Salzman, Eric. *Twentieth-Century Music: An Introduction*. Prentice-Hall, 1967.

Wilder, Robert. *Twentieth-Century Music*. Brown, 1969.

## Score and Record Anthologies

Historical anthologies in score listed here are indicated by (S) following the title; record anthologies are indicated by (R) following the title; and combined score and record anthologies are indicated by (SR).

Davison, Archibald T., and Willi Apel. *Historical Anthology of Music* (S). 2 vols. Harvard University Press, 1950. Vol. 1, from antiquity to the end of the Renaissance; Vol. 2, baroque and classical eras. Each volume has commentaries and text translations in the back.

*History of European Music* (R). The Musical Heritage Society. Orpheus Series. Three LP discs (OR349/351), recording numbers 9 through 41 of the *Historical Anthology of Music* (S), have been issued to date.

*Historical Anthology of Music* (R). Pleiades Records. Five LP discs (P250/254), recording numbers 42 through 139 of the *Historical Anthology of Music* (S), have been issued to date.

Hardy, Gordon, and Arnold Fish. *Music Literature* (S). 2 vols. Dodd, Mead, 1966. Vol. 1, mostly homophonic music in various media; Vol. 2, polyphony from the 9th to the 20th centuries.

*The History of Music in Sound* (R). RCA and Oxford University Press. Ten boxed volumes of discs; descriptive booklets in each box. This anthology is intended to accompany *The New Oxford History of Music*.

Lerner, Edward. *Study Scores of Musical Styles* (S). McGraw-Hill, 1968. Eighty-six complete examples of music from plainsong to Bach; descriptive commentaries and translations of texts.

Parrish, Carl, and John Ohl. *Masterpieces of Music Before 1750* (SR). Norton, 1951. A concise anthology of 50 representative examples of music from plainsong through the Baroque, with commentaries and text translations. Authentic recordings of the music issued by Haydn Society HSE 9038/9040.

Parrish, Carl. *A Treasury of Early Music* (SR). Norton, 1958. A companion anthology to the above work. Recording: Haydn Society HSE 9100/9103.

Schering, Arnold. *Geschichte der Musik in Beispielen* (S). Breitkopf & Härtel, 1931. Reprinted 1950 by Broude Bros. 313 examples in one volume, from antiquity to Mozart and Gluck.

Wennerstrom, Mary. *Anthology of Twentieth-Century Music* (S). Appleton-Century-Crofts, 1969. Twenty-three compositions representing various styles, media, and composers of the 20th century. Brief biographical and analytical commentaries.

### Notation

Apel, Willi. *The Notation of Polyphonic Music, 900–1600.* 5th ed. Cambridge, Mass.: The Medieval Academy, 1961.

Parrish, Carl. *The Notation of Medieval Music.* Norton, 1957.

### Pictures

Baines, Anthony. *European and American Musical Instruments.* Batsford, 1966.

Kinsky, Georg. *A History of Music in Pictures.* Dutton, 1937.

### Theoretical Writing

Phelps, Norman. "Theory, musical," in *Harvard Dictionary of Music,* p. 844 ff.

Strunk, Oliver. *Source Readings in Music History from Classical Antiquity through the Romantic Era.* Norton, 1950; issued in four paperback volumes, 1965. Translations of important writings of theorists.

# *Glossary*

A Cappella. Choral music without instrumental accompaniment.

Accent. Emphasis placed on a tone or chord.

Accidental. A sharp, flat, or natural sign.

Accompaniment. Subordinate harmonic and/or rhythmic material supporting a principal melody.

Air. A vocal or instrumental melody.

Ambitus. The range of a plainsong from its highest to its lowest tone.

Anticipation. An unaccented nonharmonic tone which resolves by repetition.

Antiphonal. Alternating choirs.

Aria. A solo song in an opera, oratorio, or cantata.

Arpeggio. The notes of a chord played consecutively in a consistently ascending or descending direction.

Atonality. Absence of key or central tonality.

Augmentation. To double the note values of a melody.

Augmented Triad. A three-note chord consisting of two major thirds.

Authentic Cadence. A cadence concluding with the progression dominant to tonic (V I).

Authentic Mode. In plainsong, a mode which ranges above the final.

Auxiliary Tone. An unaccented nonharmonic tone approached step-wise from above or below a chordal tone to which it returns.

Ayre. A song or polyphonic vocal composition; old English spelling of air.

Band. A large ensemble consisting mainly of wind instruments.

Bar, Barline. A vertical line drawn through one or more staves to indicate a measure. Bar also means measure (e.g., a four-bar phrase).

BAR FORM. A form in three sections, the first of which is repeated (*AAB*).

BASS. A voice, instrument, or part in the low register.

BASSO CONTINUO. The instrumental figured-bass part in an ensemble, played by one or more bass instruments and a keyboard instrument.

BASSO OSTINATO. A persistently repeated theme in the bass register.

BEAT. The unit of time in metric music. In time signatures, the upper numeral indicates the number of beats per measure.

BINARY. A form in two sections (*AB*).

BITONALITY. Use of two different keys simultaneously.

BRASS. Wind instruments which produce tone by vibration of the lips.

BROKEN CHORD. The tones of a chord played consecutively, usually according to some pattern.

CADENCE. The harmonic or melodic progression which concludes a phrase, section, or composition.

CAMBIATA. In the Renaissance, an unaccented nonharmonic tone approached downward by step and resolved, on downward, by skip of a third to a chordal tone, followed by stepwise upward progression.

CANON. Contrapuntal form in which the entire melodic line in one part is strictly imitated in one or more other parts at fixed intervals of pitch and time.

CANTABILE. In a singing style.

CANTUS FIRMUS. A "borrowed" melody (plainsong, chorale, folk tune) to which other melodic lines are added in a contrapuntal texture.

CHAMBER MUSIC. An ensemble consisting of only a few instruments and usually only one instrument to a part.

CHANSON. French term for song.

CHANT. General term for liturgical song similar to plainsong.

CHOIR. Vocal ensemble, usually small church choruses. Also applied to groups in an orchestra: e.g., brass choir, woodwind choir.

CHORAL. Music for chorus or choir.

CHORALE. German hymn.

CHORALE PRELUDE. Organ composition based on a chorale melody.

CHORD. A combination of three or more tones.

CHORDAL STYLE. In vocal polyphony, a texture in which all the parts have the same rhythm and sing the same syllables simultaneously. Also called familiar style.

CHORUS. A large vocal ensemble.

CHROMATIC, CHROMATICISM. Extensive use of accidentals in melody and harmony.

CHROMATIC SCALE. Twelve consecutive tones within an octave, one half step apart.

COLORATION. Written-out ornamentation.

COLORATURA. A vocal style involving light and fast scales, arpeggios, and ornaments. Also, a soprano voice capable of singing such music.

CONJUNCT. Stepwise progression in melody.

CONSONANCE, CONSONANT. Harmonic intervals (thirds, forths, fifths, sixths, and octaves) which produce a sense of repose; harmony which consists only or mainly of these intervals.

COUNTERPOINT, CONTRAPUNTAL. Texture consisting of two or more independent melodic lines.

CONTRARY MOTION. Simultaneous melodic progression in opposite direction between two parts.

CRESCENDO. Increasing the dynamic levels; getting louder.

DA CAPO. To return to the beginning of a composition. Abbreviation: D.C.

DIATONIC. Melody or harmony confined to the tones of the scale; the opposite of chromatic.

DIMINISHED TRIAD. A three-note chord consisting of two minor thirds.

DIMINUENDO. Decreasing the dynamic level; getting softer.

DIMINUTION. To halve the note values of a melody. Also, a form of ornamentation.

DISJUNCT. Melodic progression dominated by wide skips.

DISSONANCE, DISSONANT. Harmonic intervals (seconds, sevenths, ninths, augmented and diminished intervals) which produce the effect of action or tension; chords which contain one or more of these intervals.

DOMINANT. The fifth tone of a diatonic scale, and the chord built on that tone.

DOTTED RHYTHM. Rhythmic patterns consisting of a dotted note followed by a note of the next smaller denomination (e.g., a dotted quarter followed by an eighth note).

DOUBLE BAR. Two vertical lines drawn through one or more staves to indicate a major sectional division or the conclusion of a composition.

DOUBLE FUGUE. A fugue with two subjects and, correspondingly, two expositions.

DOUBLE STOPPING. Playing two notes simultaneously on a bowed string instrument.

DUPLE METER. Two or four beats to the measure.

DYNAMICS. Levels of soft and loud.

EIGHTH NOTE. One eighth the value of a whole note ($\flat$).

ELEVENTH CHORD. A chord of six tones, five superimposed thirds.

EMBELLISHMENT. Short, fast ornaments such as trills, mordents, and turns.

ENSEMBLE. A performing group consisting of two or more players or singers.

ETHNOMUSICOLOGY. The study of music of different cultures, especially non-Western or non-European music.

FAMILIAR STYLE. Chordal style in polyphonic music.

FAUXBOURDON. Parallel first inversion chords in 15th-century music.

FIGURATION. Recurrent melodic pattern.

FIGURED BASS. Use of numerals and other signs accompanying the notes of a bass part to indicate harmony to be filled in on a keyboard instrument; used in the Baroque.

FINAL. The concluding tone in a plainsong; the tonic.

FINALE. The last movement or concluding section of a large composition.

FLAT. A symbol placed in front of a note to indicate lowering that note by one half step ($\flat$).

FLORID. Ornamented, embellished, decorated.

FORM. The plan of organization of musical materials.

FORTE. Loud. Abbreviation: $f$

FUGAL. In the style of a fugue; use of contrapuntal imitation.

FUGHETTA. A short fugue or a fugal section in a composition.

FUGUE. A contrapuntal form based on imitation of a subject (theme).

GLISSANDO. Producing all pitches between two or more notes, as by sliding the finger along the string of a violin or the keyboard of a piano.

HALF NOTE. One half the value of a whole note ($\downarrow$).

HARMONY. The element of music having to do with simultaneous sounds, the combinations of tones, chord structure, chord progression, consonance, and dissonance.

HOMOPHONY, HOMOPHONIC. A texture consisting of a single melodic line with subordinate accompaniment. Also, sometimes used to mean chordal style in polyphonic music.

HYMN. A religious song.

IDIOM. Style appropriate to a specific medium, its capacities and limitations. Also used to mean style in general.

IMITATION. A theme or melody which appears consecutively in different parts in contrapuntal texture.

IMPROVISATION. To create music extemporaneously. Also applies to unindicated ornamentation and to realization of a figured bass.

INSTRUMENTATION. The instruments indicated in an orchestral score.

INTERVAL. The pitch distance between two tones, designated numerically as seconds, thirds, fourths, and so on.

INVERSION. In melody, the interval-for-interval progression in the opposite direction, up for down and vice versa. In harmony, the root of a chord in some part other than the bass, e.g., first inversion (third of the chord in the bass), second inversion (fifth of the chord in the bass).

INVERTIBLE COUNTERPOINT. Counterpoint so designed that either of two melodic lines may be the upper.

KEY. The tonal center of a composition or subdivision thereof. The key of a composition is indicated by the letter name of its tonic. Also, the white or black surface on a keyboard instrument which produces a tone when depressed.

KEYBOARD. The series of black and white keys of a piano, organ, harpsichord or similar instrument.

KEY SIGNATURE. Sharps or flats at the beginning of each staff to indicate the key of the composition.

LEADING TONE. The seventh note of a diatonic scale and the chord built on that note.

LIBRETTO. The text of an opera, oratorio, or cantata.

LIED. German word for song; plural: lieder.

LIEDERBUCH. German book of songs.

LINE. The melodic component in a composition; melodic line.

LINEAR COUNTERPOINT. Dissonant counterpoint.

LITURGICAL. Music intended for performance in a church service.

LYRIC. Song-like, as opposed to dramatic.

MAJOR. A diatonic scale with half steps between the third and fourth and between the seventh and eighth tones of the scale. Also, a triad consisting of a major and a minor third.

MEASURE. A group of beats between bar lines; also, all the notes between two bar lines.

MEDIANT. The third note of a diatonic scale, and the chord built on that note.

MEDIUM. The voices and/or instruments required for the performance of a composition; plural: media.

MELISMA, MELISMATIC. A melodic passage sung to one syllable of the text; a melodic style of many notes to a syllable.

MELODY, MELODIC. Consecutive tones; the linear or horizontal element of music.

METER, METRIC. The measuring of time in music according to a specific number of beats to the measure.

MINOR. A diatonic scale with a half step between the second and third notes of the scale; the upper tetrachord of a minor scale is variable, resulting in natural, harmonic, and melodic forms of the minor scale. A triad consisting of a minor and major third.

MODALITY, MODAL. Melody and/or harmony based on one of the church modes.

MODE. One of the eight church modes. Also refers to major or minor keys.

MODULATION. Melodic or harmonic progressions which begin in one key and end in another.

MONODY. Early 17-century term for accompanied solo songs.

MONOPHONY, MONOPHONIC. Texture consisting of a single melodic line without accompaniment.

MOTIVE. A short melodic and/or rhythmic fragment.

MOVEMENT. The complete and independent part of large works such as sonatas, symphonies, suites.

MULTITONALITY. Music which shifts abruptly between two or more remotely related keys without modulation.

MUSICOLOGY. The scholarly study of music, especially research in music history.

NATURAL. A symbol which cancels a previously indicated sharp or flat (♮).

NEIGHBOR TONE. Same as auxiliary tone.

NEOMODALITY. Modern melodic or harmonic material which makes use of a church mode or some new scale basis.

NINTH CHORD. A chord of five tones, four superimposed thirds.

NONCHORDAL, NONHARMONIC. A dissonant tone which does not belong to the chord with which it sounds.

NOTATION. Systems of symbols for writing music, mainly indicating pitch and duration of tones.

OCTAVE. The pitch interval between a tone and the seventh tone above it in a diatonic scale, or between the letter name of a tone and its recurrence above or below. The vibration ratio of an octave is two to one: if the tone A is 440 vibrations per second, the octave above it is 880 and the octave below is 220.

OPERA. A drama with music.

ORATORIO. A nonliturgical, nontheatrical religious work.

ORCHESTRA. A large instrumental ensemble.

ORCHESTRATION. The manner in which instruments are employed in an orchestral composition.

OSTINATO. A persistent rhythmic and/or melodic pattern.

OVERTURE. The instrumental introduction to an opera or oratorio.

PARALLEL KEYS. Major and minor keys having the same letter name but different key signatures (e.g., G major with one sharp and G minor with two flats).

PARALLEL MOTION, PARALLELISM. Two or more melodic lines which move simultaneously in the same direction and by the same intervals.

PART. The single line in a polyphonic composition. One refers to the soprano part, the violin part, and so on.

PASSING TONE. An unaccented nonharmonic tone between two chordal tones a third apart.

PEDAL POINT. A sustained tone in the bass over which changing harmonies take place.

PENTATONIC. A five-tone scale (e.g., the black keys of the piano).

PERCUSSION. Essentially rhythmic instruments such as drums, cymbals, gongs, and triangle.

PHRASE. A musical unit, often four measures in length, which concludes with a cadence.

PIANO. A keyboard instrument. Also, the indication for soft, a low dynamic level. Abbreviation: *p*

PICKUP BEAT. One or several unaccented notes of a melody preceding the bar line at the beginning of a phrase. Also called anacrusis.

PITCH. The vibration frequency of a tone.

PIZZICATO. Plucking the strings of a bowed string instrument.

PLAGAL CADENCE. The progression subdominant to tonic (IV I) at the conclusion of a cadence.

PLAGAL MODE. In plainsong, the modes which range approximately a fourth below and a fifth above the final.

PLAINSONG. Liturgical Catholic monophonic song. Also called Gregorian chant, plainchant.

POLYCHORAL. The use of two or more separate choirs.

POLYPHONY, POLYPHONIC. A texture consisting of two or more independent melodic lines; nearly synonymous with counterpoint, contrapuntal.

POLYTONALITY, POLYTONAL. The simultaneous use of two or more keys.

PREPARATION. A chordal (consonant) tone which subsequently becomes a nonchordal (dissonant) tone, as in a suspension.

PROGRAM MUSIC. Instrumental music which the composer intends to be descriptive of some action, scene, or story, and which carries a descriptive title.

PROGRESSION. A sequence of tones in melody, or chords in harmony.

PSALM. Musical setting of texts from the biblical Book of Psalms.

QUARTER NOTE. One fourth the value of a whole note ( ♩ ).

RANGE. The pitch distance between the highest and lowest note of a melody, voice, or instrument.

REALIZATION, TO REALIZE. Filling in the harmony of a figured bass.

RECITATIVE. A declamatory prose style of singing in operas, oratorios, and cantatas.

REFRAIN. Recurrent lines of text and music at the end of each stanza of a song.

REGISTER. The general pitch level of a part, voice, or instrument (e.g., soprano implies a high register, bass a low register).

REGISTRATION. The combinations of stops used in an organ composition.

RELATIVE KEYS. Major and minor keys which have the same key signature (e.g., C major and A minor are relative keys).

RESPONSORIAL. In plainsong, a section for solo voice followed by a section for chorus in unison.

RHYTHM. The time element in music which is determined by accent and/or duration of tones.

ROOT. The tone on which a chord is built.

SCALE. A system of adjacent notes on which melody and harmony are based.

SCORE. Two or more staves with notes vertically aligned in vocal or instrumental part music.

SEQUENCE. A recurrent melodic pattern repeated at successively higher or lower intervals. In plainsong, a form of trope.

SEVENTH CHORD. A chord of four tones, three superimposed thirds.

SFORZANDO. Suddenly loud.

SHARP. A symbol placed in front of a note to indicate raising that note by one half step (♯).

SIXTEENTH NOTE. One sixteenth the value of a whole note ( ♪ ).

SONG. A vocal solo.

SONORITY. Qualities of texture: thick or thin, heavy or light, etc.

STAFF, STAVES. The five horizontal parallel lines on or between which notes are written.

STRINGS. Instruments which produce tone by bowing or plucking taut strings (e.g., violins, guitars).

STRING QUARTET. A chamber ensemble consisting of two violins, viola, and cello. Also, compositions written for that medium.

STROPHIC. Song form in which all stanzas of the text are set to the same music.

STYLE. The characteristic quality of music determined by the integration of all elements (e.g., rhythm, melody, harmony, texture).

SUBDOMINANT. The fourth note of a diatonic scale and the chord built on that note.

SUBJECT. The theme of a fugue.

SUBMEDIANT. The sixth note of a diatonic scale and the chord built on that note.

SUITE. An instrumental composition of numerous movements, often of a dance-like character.

SUSPENSION. A nonharmonic device in which a chordal (consonant) tone is held through a change of harmony to become a non-chordal (dissonant) tone which then resolves downward to another chordal (consonant) tone.

SYLLABIC. A style of text setting in which there is a predominance of one syllable of the text to one note of the melody.

SUPERTONIC. The second note of a diatonic scale and the chord built on that note.

SYMPHONY. An orchestra, or a multimovement form for orchestra.

SYNCOPATION. A rhythmic device in which the normal accents of the measure are displaced by accenting weak beats, rests on strong beats, or tying notes over from a weak to a strong beat.

TEMPO. Generally, the speed of music; the rate of beats as indicated by such terms as allegro, presto, adagio, lento, and andante.

TERNARY. A form in three sections (*ABA*).

TETRACHORD. A four-tone section of a scale.

TEXTURE. The disposition of the melodic element in music. (See monophonic, polyphonic, homophonic); also means sonority.

THEME. The melodic idea on which a composition is based. A theme may also include rhythmic, harmonic, and other factors.

THOROUGH BASS. See basso continuo, figured bass.

TIE. A curved line connecting two consecutive notes on the same line or space of the staff; indicates the note to be held over rather than repeated.

TIMBRE. Tone color or tone quality.

TIME SIGNATURE. Numerals at the beginning of a composition, the upper figure of which indicates the number of beats in the measure, the lower of which indicates the kind of note which gets one beat.

TONALITY. The sense of gravitation around a tonal center or key.

TONIC. The first note of a diatonic scale, the note from which a key gets its name, and the chord built on that note.

TRANSCRIPTION. Arranging a composition for a different medium.

TREBLE. A relatively high-register part, indicated by the G clef or treble clef.

TREMOLO. Rapid reiteration of a sing-note or rapid alternation between two notes.

TRIAD. A three-note chord, consisting of two thirds.

TRIPLE METER. Three beats to the measure.

TRIPLE STOPPING. Playing on three strings of a bowed string instrument, simultaneously or in rapid succession.

TROPE. An interpolated section of melody and text in plainsong.

TUNE. A melody.

TUTTI. A passage played by the entire orchestra.

UNACCOMPANIED. A solo part, passage, or vocal ensemble without accompaniment.

UNISON. Two parts singing or playing the same note.

VARIATION. The modified repetition of a theme or melody; a form based on this technique.

VIRTUOSITY. Prominent display of technical facility in performance.

VOCAL. Music to be performed by the human voice or voices.

VOICE. The human organ of sound, classified according to registers (e.g., soprano, alto, tenor, bass). Also, a part in polyphonic music (e.g., a four-voice madrigal, a five-voice fugue).

WHOLE NOTE. The basic unit of note values ( o ).

WHOLE-TONE SCALE. A scale of six notes a whole step apart.

WIND INSTRUMENTS. Instruments which produce tones by a vibrating column of air when blown; woodwinds and brass.

WOODWIND INSTRUMENTS. Wind instruments which generate tone by a vibrating reed (e.g., oboes, clarinets, saxophones, bassoons) or by a whistle-type mechanism (flutes, recorders).

# Index